A book on missional intentionality that doesn't lose sight of the atoning work of Christ is what we needed in this conversation about what it means to be "for the city." I am grateful for both Darrin and Matt for helping us see through so many of the hollow "slippery slope" arguments on this subject. You should read this book!

Matt Chandler, lead pastor, The Village Church

I never expected to fight back tears as I read a book on urban church life, but I did as I read this book. I couldn't help but imagine a leader reading this book and finding the charge to immerse himself in a city for the sake of the kingdom. The very thought of it all struck me as to how Christ is still building his church, still uprooting the powers, still reigning from the heavenly places. The book is aflame with Christ, his gospel, his love for the city, his mercy to the poor. If you're tired of the same old models and the same old discussions, and if you're ready to join Jesus in something different, something dangerous, read this book.

—Russell D. Moore, Dean,
The Southern Baptist Theological Seminary

Darrin Patrick and Matt Carter not only have a heart for the city; they also know how to actually impact a city—and that's a far more difficult thing to do. You'll find their story, the values behind their story, their transparency, and practical advice to be transformative no matter where God has placed you or called you to bring glory to his name.

—Larry Osborne, author and pastor,

North Coast Church, Vista, CA

My two friends Darrin and Matt have written an interesting and informative book on how to reach the "CITY" wherever it is with a gospel-centric approach to teaching and a sensitivity to the needs of that city's culture. Well done! The book could be an outline for future church plants on how to be effective for the cause of Christ in cities all over the world.

—Billy Hornsby, president of ARC,
Association of Related Churches.

For too long churches have seen the city as their resource for growth rather than the church as the resource for the city. Matt and Darrin are two young pastors who have with sound theology and deliberate practice lived out what "missional" truly is all about. I have followed both of them for years. It's not just talk with them, but it's real and it's what their churches are all about.

—Bob Roberts, Jr., senior pastor, NorthWood Church;
author: *Transformation, Real Time Connections*

The Austin Stone has been one of the most exciting things to happen to the city of Austin in my thirteen years here. Its impact on the city, the University of Texas, my team, and my family is immeasurable. Read Matt and Darrin's book to see why.

—Rick Barnes, head coach, University of Texas Basketball

I picked this book up, started reading it, and did not put it down until I finished it. Darrin and Matt have written a book that is interesting and insightful. It is brutally honest and transparent as they share their successes and failures, the highs and lows of planting a church and going hard in ministry. The goal of the book is that readers will "catch a vision of biblical ministry, ministry done by churches that preach and serve as Jesus intended." They have succeeded.

—Dr. Daniel L. Akin, president,
Southeastern Baptist Theological Seminary

I've had the unique opportunity of being a part of both the Austin Stone and The Journey in St. Louis. Learning from both Darrin and Matt has been a huge blessing. These are amazing men of God, whom I look up to and admire. This book is a must read for anybody looking to grow in their Christian walk.

—Matt Holliday, left fielder for the St Louis Cardinals

For the City is that rare work of missiology that is both biblical and evangelical but also uniquely confessional. It should be required reading for every aspiring church planter and for those interested in gospel-powered transformation in the modern world.

—Jared C. Wilson, pastor and author of *Your Jesus Is Too Safe*

Biblical. Practical. Insightful. In *For the City*, you will find all three—a rare, refreshing triple play in a book on church ministry. If you want to reach the urban masses with the Word of God—read this book, reflect on its truths, and apply it to your ministry.

—Dr. James MacDonald, senior pastor of Harvest Bible Chapel

The Journey has been pivotal in the maturing of my faith and coming to truly understand the gospel. As a result of that, I have been more confident in sharing my faith and explaining who God is and what he's done on the platform he gave me. The Journey has also shown me what it is to be communal and actually love a city, not just spiritually but physically and materially. I highly recommend this book if you want to be challenged to love your city better.

—Mark Clayton, wide receiver, St. Louis Rams

FOR
THE
CITY

EXPONENTIAL series

Proclaiming and Living Out the Gospel

FOR THE CITY

Darrin Patrick and Matt Carter

with Joel A. Lindsey

ZONDERVAN®

EXPONENTIAL network

Leadership Network®

ZONDERVAN.com/
AUTHORTRACKER
follow your favorite authors

ZONDERVAN

For the City
Copyright © 2010 by Matt Carter and Darrin Patrick, with Joel Lindsey

This title is also available as a Zondervan ebook. Visit www.zondervan.com/ebooks.

This title is also available in a Zondervan audio edition. Visit www.zondervan.fm.

Requests for information should be addressed to:

Zondervan, *Grand Rapids, Michigan 49530*

Library of Congress Cataloging-in-Publication Data

Patrick, Darrin, 1970-
　　　For the city : proclaiming and living out the Gospel / Darrin Patrick and Matt
　　Carter with Joel Lindsey.
　　　　　　p.　cm. — (Exponential series)
　　　　ISBN　978-0-310-33007-3 (softcover)
　　　　1. City churches. 2. City missions. I. Carter, Matt, 1973- II. Lindsey, Joel.
　　III. Title. IV. Title: Proclaiming and living out the Gospel.
　　BV637.P38　2010
　　254'.5091732 — dc22　　　　　　　　　　　　　　　　　　　　　2010052440

Agent line goes here if needed.

Cover design: Studio Gearbox
Interior design: Sherri L. Hoffman

Printed in the United States of America

11 12 13 14 15 16 /DCI/ 22 21 20 19 18 17 16 15 14 13 12 11 10 9 8 7 6 5 4 3 2 1

I could not have written this book without the daily support
of my godly wife, Amie, and our city-loving kids:
Glory, Gracie, Drew, and Lainey.
–D. P.

For my earthly father. You bear the name
of the disciple Jesus loved.
You bear it well.
–M. C.

Principal among the blessings in my life is my wife, Melissa.
She is a treasure in which I rejoice and at the same
time continue to dig for. I love a good treasure hunt!
–J. L.

Finally, this book is dedicated to Austin, Texas,
and St. Louis, Missouri,
two of the greatest cities in God's world.

Contents

Acknowledgments

The elders, members, and partners of the Journey and Austin Stone Community Church have taught us pretty much everything we know about doing ministry for our cities. These people have forced us to move from theories of ministry to the practice of ministry, and through them God has shaped us in ways we won't ever fully know.

Darrin: I am thankful to all of my ministry mentors whom God used to equip me over the years: Bob Wagner, Ray Kirk, Joe Wagner, Rob Landes, Wayne Barber, Becky Castle, Rick McGinniss, and Kitti Homan. Special thanks goes to Dr. Tim Keller, who has been a voice of challenge for me to give my life to ministry for the sake of cities.

Matt: I am grateful for my greatest ministry mentor and partner, my wife, Jennifer. I would also like to thank Bob Swan, who mentored me while I was a youth pastor; Chris Osborne, who gave me a passion for the Word of God and expositional preaching; Chris Tomlin, who forced me to think about city ministry when I was thinking suburbs; and Louie Giglio, who taught me the value of Christ-centered, God-exalting worship. I also want to say a special thanks to Glenn Lucke, who was invaluable to me during the writing process.

Finally, this book was written with Joel Lindsey, pastor of theology and care at The Journey. During the writing process he emerged as much more than a content editor. He not only unified the separate voices in this volume, but also provided helpful insights and much of the content you find here. This book simply would not exist without his dedication to the Lord, the church, and the topics we explore here.

Foreword

Greater things are yet to come...

It's interesting to be writing a foreword for a book about the church "for the city," considering I grew up in a small East Texas town. To me, the city was any place that had a Wal-Mart or a McDonalds. I am extremely thankful and proud of the little place I called home for the first half of my life. And it was the church in this town that was so pivotal as a foundation for my faith. Little did I know, since those days, I would travel around the world a few times and have my eyes opened and mind blown at the diversity of this world and yet the connectedness of it.

I love that this book is targeted to the cities — a book about what it looks like to lead the church in the city. I now call Atlanta home. It's a massive place. And while I will never get used to planning my days around traffic jams, I count it a privilege to be a part of a church community in such a diverse city. The cities of the world are the influencers. What begins on the eight-lane highway will eventually find its way to the Farm to Market road.

The city is a place of opportunity. It's where most teenagers want to find themselves some day. The city is full of energy and culture. And in the city you find the most beautiful churches in the world — though sadly, many are just architectural works of art now. Most of the seats, once filled, sit empty on Sunday mornings and throughout the week. Regretfully, those spires and steeples have lost their influence.

However, it's a new day. I believe wholeheartedly that greater things are yet to come and greater things are still to be done. The church is God's Plan A, and there is no Plan B. Maybe you've heard it several times, but it needs to be continually said, the church is not a building; rather, it's God's people, his sons and daughters. That's right, the church is on your street... because you are on your street. Yes, cities can be intimidating. People are everywhere. And with mass humanity comes mass brokenness. And into the chaos stands the church, the light of the world. There is nothing more exciting or rewarding than to know you are a part of God's mission. It's humbling to think we are his hands and feet.

Most of all, the church is for God. Of course, you might say, "Duh!" But if you look at many of our gatherings, you might think we are more concerned how the congregation feels about things than how God might actually feel about them.

This is ultimately what these coming pages are about. I know the heart of Matt and Darrin. I've even had the privilege to come alongside Matt as we ventured into Austin to plant an expression of what is written in this book. One thing I know—no one is keeping score. God is not holding a report card over our head. It's not about getting it perfectly right. No need to read this book through any kind of "Do I measure up?" lens. God is still looking for hearts that are completely his. It's that simple. I trust this book to you. Both of these men have great hearts after God and a passion to see God's glory in their cities.

Yes, greater things are still to be done in our cities!

—Chris Tomlin

Why a Church
For the City?

What makes a great church?
That's a question all Christians should ask themselves.
Not just pastors, not just worship leaders, not just the most gifted
volunteers, but every Christian. And we need to be asking this
question because God has some specific ideas about what it means
to be a great church.

Many of us think we go to a great church. After all, nobody
ever sets out on a spiritual journey to find the most mediocre,
lukewarm church around. No, when most of us describe a great
church, a successful church, what we are really talking about is
a church that meets our needs. The church has preaching that
makes us feel good or challenges us just a little, but not too much.
The music is pleasing to us, meaning the church has drums or
doesn't have drums (depending on which we prefer). The church
has a program or two that is right up our alley and makes us feel
as if we have a place to serve.

And there is nothing wrong with good preaching, good music,
and well-run programs.

But these things do not define a successful church. We are on
dangerous ground when we seek to define the worth of a church
by how it meets our felt needs. Instead, we have to start defining
success of a church based on God's criteria. Then we don't run the
risk of spending every Sunday for the rest of our lives completely
missing the heart of God.

A great church, a healthy church, is one in which Jesus Christ
is found in word and deed. The emphasis here is on the word

"and." A healthy church isn't just a preaching church. A successful church isn't simply a hub for social justice. A God-honoring, gospel-loving church is one where the Word of God is the primary motivator for doing the work of God.

Great churches have some distinguishing characteristics, and over the next 150 or so pages, we hope to not only shed light on what a healthy church looks like, but share from our experiences as church planters how to pursue the goal of healthy, God-honoring churches in cities that desperately need gospel transformation. Along the way you'll learn about us—who we are and how we got to our cities.

You'll hear from Matt as he describes his conversion from a sheltered, church-going boy to a sold-out, gospel-loving man surrendered to God's call to plant a church in a diverse, artistic, and just plain weird city like Austin, Texas.

You'll also hear from Darrin, who was plucked from a life of drug and alcohol abuse and boundary-less sexual relationships because God had plans for his life that included planting a church in a racially divided, working-class, rust-belt city like St. Louis, Missouri.

In this book we will explore what it means to be a church for the city God has called you to engage. If you are a church planter, we hope you will learn as much from our mistakes, some of which are outlined in chapter 9, as you learn from our successes.

If you are a pastor or staff member at an existing church in your city, we hope you will be challenged to resubmit your church plans and programs to the Lord and analyze them again through the filter of the gospel, emboldened to fertilize and grow the ministries that will bear fruit, and prune the ministries that are hindering the efforts to reach your city.

If you are a Christian seeking to move from member to missionary, we hope you will be encouraged by what you find here. We want to present you with stories, tips, tools, and questions that help you think through what God is calling you, as an individual and as a member of the body of Christ, to do about your city's need for the gospel.

For all who are reading this book, we pray that God will inspire you to rethink what it means to be part of something bigger than yourself, part of a gospel movement in your city where the good news of Jesus' life, death, and resurrection is proclaimed, the poor and marginalized are empowered, and the God of the Bible is seen as the God of your city.

Part 1

A TALE OF TWO CITIES

CHAPTER 1

Gospel-Centered City Ministry (Matt)

In the fall of 2001 I (Matt) went through the church planter assessment process with the Southern Baptists of Texas Convention (SBTC). At the time, the SBTC was taking a critical look at various church planting models, debating the merits and pitfalls of each. The sample of church models included the "Willow Creek model," the "Saddleback" or "Purpose-Driven model," and what people then referred to as the "Andy Stanley model." These were all variants of a generalized "seeker model" of planting a church.[1]

If you were thinking about being a church planter, or at least a successful church planter, you selected one of the major models. You crafted a prospectus based on one of the models. If you were approved in the assessment process, you then traveled to the city to which you were called, set up shop, and executed this model in your city. If a church plant was going to succeed, it was going to do so based on how well it adhered to the model it was based on. Rinse, repeat step one.

In my initial meetings with the SBTC church planter assessment team, they asked me which model I was planning to follow. And they didn't just ask me once. I remember being asked a handful of times to name my preferred model. Each time, I resisted an answer, not out of arrogance, but because the idea of selecting a model prior to moving to Austin didn't make sense to me. After

---

1. For the record, Matt and Darrin believe that seeker churches have been and continue to be used by God to reach the lost in their cities and also to wake the church up to the need to reach those who are far from God.

all, the Lord led me to Austin, and through much thought and prayer, he instructed me to get to know the people of Austin, their needs and unique cultural expressions, before developing a detailed plan of action. I wanted to go back to the Scriptures. I wanted to study Acts. I wanted to immerse myself in the Scriptures in order to understand more deeply the values and related principles of a New Testament church.[2]

In essence, I thought the SBTC guys—who are great guys and helped me enormously in many ways—focused first on the pragmatics of models while I wanted to focus first on the principles in Scripture. Both are necessary, but it seemed wise to me to be biblically and theologically driven first, deriving pragmatic applications from the Scriptures, church history, and sound doctrine.

During our conversations, the assessment team and I had open and honest debate about an appropriate philosophy of ministry. Our interactions were friendly and loving, not adversarial. The SBTC guys were (and still are) on my team, just as I was (and still am) on their team. We dialogued as brothers committed to Christ and the mission of his church.

All of my conversation with them, though, came down to one piece of advice and one basic question: "We think you should have a model. Which one will you choose?"

So I gave in. Sort of.

I replied, "You want a model? Here it is.

"Imagine an urban church so influenced by the power of the gospel that it seized every opportunity to proclaim and live out the gospel for the good of the city. Imagine that this church physically and spiritually served the poorest of the poor, but also lovingly rebuked the wealthy. Imagine this church as the epicenter of straight-up, God-fearing, Spirit-filled revival, leading thousands of people to eternal life in Christ in just a few years. Imagine a church that built elderly housing, housed all the orphans in the

---

2. A great reference for the theology and missiology of the New Testament church is Dean Flemming's *Contextualization in the New Testament: Patterns for Theology and Mission* (Downers Grove, IL: InterVarsity Press, 2005).

city, and taught wealthy business people to have a 'double bottom line' so they could run a profitable business in order to support the work of the church and meet the needs of the city.

"In other words, imagine a church that boldly preached the gospel and lived out the values of the kingdom. Don't you want to be a part of a church like that?"

"Of course. Who wouldn't?" they responded.

"What if I told you that the church model I'm describing is as trusted, tried, and true as any you'll find?" I said.

"What model is it?"

"Metropolitan Tabernacle," I replied, receiving blank stares in return.

"Where is it? Who's the pastor?" one team member asked.

A thin smile spread across my face

"London, 1852," I said. "The pastor is Charles Spurgeon."

Metropolitan Tabernacle

For those who may not be familiar with Charles Spurgeon or his church, a bit of background may be necessary.

The Industrial Revolution began in the United Kingdom in the latter half of the eighteenth century, and by the 1850s its effects pervaded England. In this period of great industrialization people left the farms and small towns and flocked to London, Manchester, and other cities. As people congregated in vast numbers, the old infrastructure of London lacked the capacity and resources to attend to the needs of the new crowds. The influx of people into London meant not only a spike in laborers and factories, but also the number of under-resourced women, children, orphans, and widows exploded in London.

The city was in crisis. The leaders didn't know what to do. They saw the mountain of needs that confronted them from every angle. Thus, in the 1850s a lot of London churches did what a lot of American churches have done during the last thirty years: they fled the cities. These churches moved their locations to the outskirts of London. But Metropolitan Tabernacle, pastored by

Charles Spurgeon, decided, "We're not going to do that. We're going to stay here. We see this as an opportunity for the gospel."[3]

Metropolitan Tabernacle looked at the needs of the people in the city and began to engage in helping them with their problems. The problems of the desperately poor were the most pressing, so Metropolitan Tabernacle leaders created almshouses for people who lost their jobs and needed time to get back on their feet. The poorhouses in London operated in terrible conditions, but the almshouses of Metropolitan Tabernacle provided a crucial alternative. The church also built a large number of homes for the elderly where they would care for them and help them die with dignity and in peace. The church created an orphanage where they educated, cared for, and fed thousands of orphans. They created homes for single mothers who had lost their husbands and helped them find employment. Metropolitan Tabernacle started a school for pastors from rural areas to receive a theological education and helped clothe and provide books for these impoverished pastors. They started programs for businessmen to use their entrepreneurial efforts to expand the kingdom through their businesses.

Metropolitan Tabernacle's influence spread so quickly throughout the poor and all the way up the class ladder to the aristocracy. It got to the point that if Metropolitan Tabernacle had shut down at any point during that decade of grappling with the problems of the Industrial Revolution, the city of London would have been crippled. They would have *grieved* the loss of the Tabernacle. Can you imagine serving the needs of the city, being so attuned to the common good for the sake of the gospel, that your city would grieve if you picked up and left?

With all of this focus on serving the poor and meeting the needs of people, you might be wondering, "Did Spurgeon ignore the preaching of the gospel?" The answer is clear: absolutely not! So many people began coming to the church, including many lost people who had never attended a church, that Spurgeon asked his

---

3. A wonderful, surprisingly brief biography of Spurgeon is Arnold A. Dallimore's, *Spurgeon: A New Biography* (Carlisle, PA: Banner of Truth, 1985).

Christian members not to attend worship once a month so the lost people would have space to come. Spurgeon saw five thousand people coming to worship at the church *each week*, and his collections of sermons are regarded as some of the finest gospel preaching ever published.

What Spurgeon and the Metropolitan Tabernacle did that was so radical and unique was to seize the opportunity all around them afforded by the needs of the people of London. It was a ministry to *all* people, and ultimately the ministry pulled in not just the poor but also the wealthy and influential.

So that's what I told my church planting friends and "mentors": "That's my model — Spurgeon and the Metropolitan Tabernacle — preach the gospel, meet the needs of the city, especially the poor."

And that's what we started doing.

Seeking the Welfare of the City

Two great Old Testament prophets can teach us a lot about how to reach our cities. Both Jonah and Jeremiah knew what it meant to be strangers in a strange land, which is exactly what Christians are. As C. S. Lewis notes in *Mere Christianity*, "If I find in myself a desire which no experience in this world can satisfy, the most probable explanation is that I was made for another world."[4] Jonah and Jeremiah, however, addressed people living in Assyria and Babylon respectively. Both of these men of God teach us important principles regarding the way God's people are to seek the welfare of their city. We'll spend a great deal of time unpacking Jonah's lessons to us in the final chapter of this book. For now, let's learn from Jeremiah.

Tim Keller, the senior pastor of Redeemer Presbyterian Church in New York City, often talks about the importance of seeking the shalom of the city. In fact, it was Keller's teaching on

---

4. C. S. Lewis, *Mere Christianity* (San Francisco: HarperCollins, 2001), 136 – 37.

Jeremiah 29 that first helped me to understand that the church does not exist to simply "fix" problems. Instead, the church is to carry the burdens of the world to Jesus. Let me explain.

In Jeremiah 29, many of the people of Judah are exiles in Babylon, the capital city of their enemies. The Lord comes to his people through the pen of Jeremiah and says, "Seek the shalom of your enemies. Seek the welfare of your captors. Sink down roots. Build houses. Plant gardens and eat. Take wives and have children. Give yourself to the prosperity of your captors in Babylon and you will have prosperity" (cf. Jer. 29:4 – 9).

American Christians, when they hear the word "shalom" or "peace," think that the word means something like "the end of war" or is the way one hippie greets another. But that's only a sliver of its fuller meaning.

Shalom is much richer than the absence of conflict or a trendy way to say good-bye. Biblical shalom connotes universal human flourishing. By seeking the shalom of the city, God was asking those in Babylonian captivity to live and invest in the midst of the social and cultural world of their enemies, encouraging and supporting the goodness and enjoyment of life by creating shalom in every niche of society.

As churches seek to embrace this call to promote human flourishing in every area of society, there are typically four approaches that they follow:

Church IN the City

There are churches that are merely *in* the city. Their heartbeat is to get people in the doors to hear the gospel. That's a good goal. But, unfortunately, that's often where it ends. Such churches create programs for people inside the church walls, and the reach of their ministry only *occasionally* goes outside to the city. The primary focus of these churches is what happens inside the church building. Churches like this are geographically *in* the city, but they aren't effectively engaged with the people and culture of the city.

Church AGAINST the City

Churches of this type have adopted a defensive posture toward the city. These churches are often located in urban areas, but everything about the surrounding culture is seen as not just bad, but irredeemable. The arts, the business world, and the media are minions of Satan bent on destroying the church. Believers in these churches often align themselves squarely against the culture and proclaim that they are taking a stand for Christ. A church *against* its city says:

Politics? Bad.

Arts? Bad.

Media? Bad.

Church? Good.

Certainly, there can be good intentions in a church like this, and there is often an authentic desire among these churches' members to avoid what is evil and cling to what is good. Faithful Christians are continually forced to think critically about what to accept and reject within the prevailing culture.

But a church *against* its city settles, even prefers, an "Us vs. Them" mentality.

Church OF the City

If churches against the city are defensive and antagonistic toward the surrounding culture, churches *of* the city go to the opposite extreme. These churches wholeheartedly embrace the culture of the city, so much so that they lose the flavor in their salt and the brightness of their light by abandoning the call to be *in* the world without being *of* the world. They bend so far to the culture that they lose their distinctive Christian identity — they lose their ability to speak truth effectively.

The loss of godly distinctiveness in an ungodly culture is not a new phenomenon. This was the primary problem with the people of Israel on their way from Egypt to the Promised Land. Moreover, in Amos 5, God acknowledges that the Israelites were following him. But both their obedience and their witness had been undercut by their loss of godly distinctiveness. Instead of faithfully worshiping the only true God, they worshiped "Sikkuth your king, and Kiyyun your star-god—your images that you made for yourselves" (Amos 5:26). Sikkuth and Kiyyun are Assyrian idols. The people of Israel had become a church *of* the city.

Church FOR the City

While each of these first three church examples highlights a negative aspect of involvement with the surrounding culture, there is a model of engagement where a church speaks the truth of the gospel and is not afraid to uphold a biblical worldview and moral standard. Such a church proclaims the truths of Scripture with passion, clarity, and boldness. At the same time, though, this is a church that commits itself to seeking the shalom, the flourishing, of the city. This means seeking the shalom of the people they live in community with, living sacrificially and using their gifts, time, and money to seek the peace and prosperity of their neighbors.

Sounds like a great idea, right?

But how does a church like that become a reality? That's what we hope to show you in this book. For the next nine chapters, Darrin and I are going to flesh out how you can be a church that boldly and faithfully proclaims the gospel *and* engages your community with acts of service and mercy.

As pastors and church planters, we have lived out these ideas in the context of city ministry. Cities are at the epicenter of God's earthshaking movements today, and it's important that any model for starting new churches takes into account the unique nuances of ministry in an urban context. But for those of you who aren't located in a larger city, many of the concepts we discuss will work equally well where you are. Much of what we show and tell in this book is transferable, from an urban church in New York City to a village in West Africa.

Anyone who has studied history and the work of God over the centuries knows that what we are talking about is nothing new. After all, Charles Spurgeon was doing much of this more than 150 years ago. But these ideas didn't originate with Spurgeon either. Jesus, when he designed and instituted his church, told them to "let your light shine before others, so that they may see your good works and give glory to your Father who is in heaven" (Matt. 5:16).

Believe us when we say that we didn't write this book so people would start more cool, hip, trendy, and relevant churches. That's not what either of us wants for the congregations we shepherd in Austin, Texas, and St. Louis, Missouri. What we want is for you, the reader, to catch a vision of biblical ministry, ministry done by churches that preach and serve as Jesus intended. We hope and pray that by God's grace you'll be inspired to plant and lead churches that recognize and seize the opportunities existing within your own city and cultural context. We want to see an increase in churches that don't separate their theology from real world social, economic, and cultural influence. Inspired by Metropolitan Tabernacle and other gospel-centered churches that have served and met the spiritual and physical needs of people, we want to have a lasting impact in our cities.

We want to be able to answer the following questions in a God-honoring way. If Austin Stone Community Church and The Journey shut our doors tomorrow, would our cities even know we were gone? Would the city leaders celebrate, feeling as if they had gotten rid of a nuisance? Or would the city grieve and mourn our disappearance?

We want our churches to be places where Jesus is preeminent, God's presence is obvious, and there is no doubt in anyone's mind … that we *love* our cities.

We want your church to be that place too.

CHAPTER 2

Planting in Mid-America (Darrin)

I (Darrin) grew up in a small rural community that had nearly as many cats as people, in a home where neither of my parents or extended family had much use for church, God, or the Bible. My dad was the hardest working man I have ever met, and not surprisingly, my two older sisters and I were instilled with the infamous Midwestern work ethic as well (evidenced by the fact that all of us had jobs before we had driver's licenses). My mom was a saint of a woman who loved her family and sought to make our home a place of peace and sanctuary. There is never a doubt in my mind that my parents loved me; their continual sacrifice and provision for me and my sisters made this abundantly clear.

Unfortunately, like most American couples,[1] my parents divorced when I was thirteen. By that time, Dad and I had drifted apart. In hindsight, and from a pastor's vantage point, I think our relationship suffered largely because our idols were incompatible. His idol was work; mine was playing sports. Right around this time I hit a growth spurt and grew larger than my mother, which, considering that Dad was not around, meant I pretty much did what I wanted when I wanted. With no dad to correct me and with my older sisters grown up and out of the house, I learned how to manipulate my mother and my "playing" turned into partying, complete with drugs, alcohol, sex, and plenty of stuff I'm sure I don't even remember and would love to forget.

---

1. According to Jennifer Baker of the Forest Institute of Professional Psychology, as of 2004, 50 percent of first marriages, 67 percent of second, and 74 percent of third marriages end in divorce. This information is available at www.divorcerate.org/.

) I was the "druggie/athlete" guy, meaning I
the football and baseball teams, but the solo
d times. I was popular because of my status as an
rence, all-regional athlete, but I was even more popular
ause I could supply the two things that most high schoolers
used to help them escape the reality of their boring, pathetic lives:
devil's brew and hippie lettuce.

Rejecting my mom's morality and my dad's hard work ethic,
I was breaking the law and taking shortcuts as a way of making
money and gaining affirmation. I'll never forget something my
mother said about me during this time. "I wouldn't be surprised if
Darrin ended up in prison or wound up dead."[2]

Conversion

For reasons that are known only to God and his heavenly coaching
staff, my high school was loaded with an unusual number of great
athletes during my time there.

In my junior year, we found ourselves fighting to win the state
playoffs. On the night of our playoff-clinching victory, several
other starters and I went out to celebrate, and I had the brilliant
idea to go into town for a little late night snack at the local Har-
dee's (or Carl's Jr. if you prefer). While we were there, I felt the call
of nature but found the bathroom door locked, and in my drunken
stupor proceeded to relieve myself at the counter as I ordered my
roast beef sandwich. The employees didn't call the cops, but they
did make me clean up my puddle. And the manager, who happened to be a booster for the football team, threw me out of his
restaurant. He placed a call to the school athletic director within
twelve hours. The next day my coach informed me I was officially
suspended for a week and unofficially for the remainder of the
season.

---

2. Ephesians 6:2–3: "'Honor your father and mother' (this is the first commandment with a promise), 'that it may go well with you and that you may live long
in the land.'"

That same week a kid smarted off to me in front of the principal's office and I gave him the "right fist of fellowship." I spent the week staring at pink walls under "in school suspension."

To top it off, during this same week my high school girlfriend told me that she was late, and she didn't mean late like she was every time we went on a date. She rejected my suggestion that she get an abortion; and though it later turned out she wasn't actually pregnant (false alarm!), the questions she began asking me and the concerns she voiced during that time of uncertainty got me thinking, for the first time in my life, about God.

In short, all my idols—everything I had trusted in for identity, significance, and security—were crumbling down around me, all in one week. God had my attention. And as only God can do, he turned my week from hell into a week from heaven.

The graduate assistant on the football team, observing that I was an angry, messed-up young man, took an interest in me. He began to pursue me, inviting me to church, and even offering to come by and drive me there. So I started going to church and hanging out with Christians for the first time in my life. And though I had ingested only one bound paper product from cover to cover (*Sports Illustrated*), I began to read my new King James Bible not only faithfully, but voraciously. I toted my leather-bound, full-name inscribed "King Jimmy" and was beginning to understand more of what Jesus had done on my behalf. Over that Christmas break, I attended my first Christian youth conference, making a commitment there to stop participating in the unholy trinity of Sex, Drugs, and Alcohol.

It lasted about twelve hours.

I woke promptly at 3:00 p.m. the next day keenly aware of the reality that no matter how hard I tried, I was not capable of following all the rules and cleaning myself up. I kept reading the Bible, and I began to understand the heart of the gospel—that it wasn't my ability and work that could save me, but it was Christ's ability and his work that could save me.

Around February of that year I became a Christian. I know

this because I began to experience conviction for sinful choices that were formerly familiar, comfortable, and enjoyable. I remember hooking up with a girl for a one-night stand and feeling bad about it. A couple of days later I got drunk at a party and was sick the whole next day. One of my buddies offered me some weed, and I said yes to getting high with him. Later that day, I got deathly ill. Now, mind you, I had never gotten sick from alcohol or drugs before, nor had I felt bad about having sex outside the covenant of marriage. For the first time in my life, I was miserable about my sin. What had happened to me that I could not enjoy what used to be my "hobbies"? Why did I keep hearing this voice saying, "This is not who you are anymore." The answer: I had been regenerated.[3]

My conversion sent shockwaves throughout my high school. Almost immediately I began to tell people that I had been changed by the power of the gospel. Most of the time this was met with skepticism. Several of my drinking and drug buddies were sad because I was no longer going to be enabling their debauchery. Others were intrigued because of my "Drugs-to-Jesus" transformation. I still attended the same parties that I always did, but now, instead of carrying a bottle or a bong, I was carrying a Bible. I would literally sit in a chair and read my Bible while everyone around me was getting wasted. More times than not I had significant spiritual conversations with partiers who were interested in what God had done in my life.

The more I read the Bible, the more I saw Jesus hanging out in the places that the pagans were, where the religious would not have been caught dead. The center of rebellion and commandment breaking in my town was a giant parking lot located near a few popular restaurants. In a stroke of creative genius, youngsters well before my era had dubbed this "The Parking Lot." Trying to

---

3. The word rendered "regeneration" in the New Testament is *palingenesia*, which literally means "new birth," or renewal. In a classical context, this word referred to changes brought about during the return of the spring season. Regeneration in Christian theology describes the heart transformation that occurs when the Spirit indwells a believer.

be like Jesus, I went to The Parking Lot and shared the gospel with anyone who would listen. I remember chasing one guy into the bathroom of one of the fast food restaurants, challenging him to repent of his sin and give his life to Christ. He did. Right there. Kneeling in a filthy, smelly bathroom, he prayed for God to have mercy on his soul. I added a prayer that God would protect him from whatever germs were present in the grime and urine that were staining the knees of his jeans.

From Ministry toward Marriage

About six months after high school graduation I met a young pastor from a neighboring town who wanted me to be his youth pastor. I thought this a weird request since I had just turned nineteen and had only been a Christian for eighteen months. He assured me that he would mentor me and that I would be OK. I accepted the position, though many of my mentors thought I shouldn't. Turns out they were right.

Not even eight months into my tenure in this church I discovered that things were not as they should be. One fateful day, I picked up the phone at the church and realized I was listening in on a conversation between the pastor and another woman in a manner that should have been reserved for his wife only. I immediately, but quietly, hung up the phone and began a secret investigation. Eventually, I tried to engage the church leadership about my concerns.

As it turned out, they were in the know about the situation and were comfortable with it because of how the pastor had helped them in "this crisis" or "that difficult time." Flabbergasted, I resigned and pulled away from ministry for a year as I tried to sort out what I had just witnessed.[4] My thought was pretty simple, "I love Jesus, but I can do without the church." And so with a love for God and indifference toward God's church, I headed off to a

---

4. Years later it was revealed that the pastor was a serial adulterer, which, thankfully, was eventually exposed.

Christian university to study the Bible and prepare for whatever it was God was calling me to do.

I arrived at Southwest Baptist University scarred from my previous ministry experience, but eager to study Greek and Hebrew. I made these languages the focus of my study. I decided that semester to become a Bible translator and go and die in some remote part of the earth translating the Scripture for some unreached people group. I wasn't really interested in the church and was less interested in becoming a pastor.

My on-and-off, post-conversion high school girlfriend, Amie, also attended SBU, having received a music scholarship. We began to date and God began to use us together to reach our friends for Christ. Because Amie was in the music program, most of her friends were artistic types. And because I was an athlete, my friends were athletic types. Amie and I would bring our respective friends, artists and athletes, to church with us. By and large, this was not a good experience for anyone involved. Her friends would comment on how poorly the music was executed, and my friends would comment on how unchallenging the pastor was. The artists were underwhelmed with the lack of transcendence and beauty in church, and the athletes were frustrated at the lack of masculinity and practicality of the Sunday experience. Over and over again we heard the same thing: our friends who were like us didn't feel like the church was for them.[5]

One day the thought occurred to me that I should start a church that my friends would actually like to attend. I knew from my theological studies that a New Testament church was to be a multiracial, multigenerational church, so it wouldn't just be a church for artists and athletes, but one where these kinds of people would feel welcome. I began to dream about this kind of church, and with equal parts excitement and fear I wondered if God would ever call me to start it.

---

5. This is not to say that there weren't some good churches in that area reaching certain kinds of people. But there was a great need for new churches reaching emerging generations in that area, and in every area for that matter.

Planting The Journey

Amie and I got married before my senior year of college (which was perfectly normal at our small, Christian college).[6] This meant I had to get a job. I was considering enrolling in seminary, something that I had been reticent to pursue in the past.[7] Around that time my supervisor in the college ministry mentioned that his friend was starting a church in Kansas City. Providentially, Rick (the guy who was starting the church) "happened" to be in the campus ministry office the very next week. After telling me the story of how he started the church, he looked at me point blank and said, "You should come and help me. You can go to seminary and start our student ministry and learn how to plant a church." It wasn't that Rick's offer to come help start a ministry with no budget and no building was that compelling, but after that conversation I had no doubt that God was calling us to move to Kansas City.

We moved in the summer after Amie graduated from college. My plan was to be in Kansas City for a couple of years. I would get the ministry started, graduate from seminary, and get all the ins and outs of church planting so that I could move to our target city, wherever that was, and do what God had called us to do. Instead, we were there six years, largely so that God could humble me and father me through the men on the staff at this new church. I had a lot to learn regarding church planting. I had even more room to grow in my character, specifically in the area of perseverance. During our time in Kansas City we were forced to learn the art of juggling many different responsibilities on little sleep and even less money. It was a wonderful and terrible time! We learned a lot about what to do in a church plant—and quite few things about what not to do as well.

---

6. See "The Case for Early Marriage," *Christianity Today*, July 31, 2009. It is available online at www.christianitytoday.com/ct/2009/august/16.22.html.

7. The main reason was that I had met people who had been to seminary. Many of them were arrogant and lacked spiritual vitality. This is in keeping with the statistics, which show that 80 percent of seminary and Bible school graduates will leave the ministry in the first five years of service. This stat is quoted in many places, including http://lamintl.org/Pastor_Statistics.aspx.

About the fifth year of our stay in Kansas City I began to get restless. I approached our pastor and asked if I could be released to plant a church. His answer was a "yes, but." Rick affirmed my gifts, but he had concerns about my administrative ability and the fact that our church didn't have money to help me go plant. He suggested that I take a sabbatical and pray for God's direction. So, I headed off to Colorado to hear from God and talk to a church planter I had met who was planting in urban Denver. I spent most of my days in the mountains and my nights talking with Pastor Ron, a church planter friend, and his family.

During one of our conversations, I remember asking him where he thought I should plant. His response was immediate: "Downtown Denver," he said. I loved the mountains, and I was feeling drawn to planting in an urban area, but at the time we were thinking somewhere in the northeast, once the buckle of the Bible belt.[8] So I asked him where else he might suggest.

He listened to my apprehensions and then asked me a question: "Where are you from?"

I answered that I was from a small, rural town in Southern Illinois that he had never heard of.

"What is the closest big city?" he asked.

I said, "St. Louis is less than a two-hour drive."

"Have you ever thought about planting in St. Louis?" I had to admit I hadn't. The thought had never crossed my mind. Pastor Ron went on to describe studies he'd read saying that the closer you grew up to the city you were planting in, the better the chance the church would survive. Now as interesting as that was, it wasn't quite as interesting as what happened next.

My Colorado trip coincided with the NFC Championship game, where the Kurt Warner-led St. Louis Rams defeated the "Aquatic Criminals"[9] from Tampa Bay en route to their first Super Bowl victory. As I was watching an interview with Warner, captain of the "Greatest Show on Turf," he began talking about how

---

8. www.tngenweb.org/campbell/hist-bogan/bible.html

9. My term of endearment for the Tampa Bay Buccaneers.

God had called him to St. Louis not just for football, but to help bring spiritual renewal to the city.

Coincidence?

I sat there stunned for a moment. I had never even considered St. Louis as an option, and now in back-to-back circumstances, the idea of being involved in the spiritual renewal of the city had come up. Could God be calling me to St. Louis? If so, when would we need to move? How would we pay for it? Would the Rams draft me as a tight end? I had many questions.

I came back to Kansas City, and my wife and a few friends began driving four hours across the nation's first interstate, I-70, to St. Louis to scout out the city and discern if we were in fact called. During these trips I interviewed pastors, and after explaining our vision I asked their opinion if a new church like that was needed. Pastor after pastor affirmed that there was a need. I was encouraged. Many of the pastors remarked at how there hadn't been a successful, nonethnic-specific church plant in a few decades. More than one pastor was brutally honest, telling me "a church like what you are talking about is needed, but I doubt it can be done."

Everything was now pointing us toward a church plant in St. Louis. Our main obstacle at that point was not a lack of vision, or a lack of training, or a lack of passion. It was a lack of money, the same concern shared by my pastor in Kansas City ... and my pregnant wife. Still, despite the lack of financing, I was determined to go, even if I had to wait tables at Applebee's (even if I had to actually eat at Applebee's).[10] We needed money, so I was willing to do whatever it took to get this church started.

This is where the story gets weird.

At about that time, my pastor in Kansas City befriended a local atheist through recreational sports. Rick began counseling this man and his wife who, like most married people, were in real need of counseling. Rick was able to help them and the couple began sporadically attending church.

---

10. Strangely, I enjoy everything listed on the menu at Applebee's. I just never seem to like the way Applebee's cooks it. Alas, it is a mystery.

Then, following a fairly routine surgery the gentleman did not come out of the anesthesia and died on the operating table. His wife and children were crushed by his death, and Rick and his wife loved and shepherded the family through this awful time, earning the family's respect and establishing a more solid relationship with the church.

Because her husband owned several businesses, the widow stood to inherit a substantial amount of money. After the widow initiated several months of conversations concerning wise use of the money, Rick asked her a simple question: "What do you want to do?" Amazingly, she responded, "I'm not sure about all the business stuff, but I want to see churches like this one get started." After that conversation, Rick immediately called me and said, "I think I have the financing that will allow you to go plant in St. Louis." And the rest is history. In June of 2001, Amie and I moved with our one-year-old daughter, Glory, to the city of St. Louis. We purchased a house where it was not uncommon to hear gunshots and where we were also "welcomed" to the neighborhood by having our car stolen within a month of our arrival.

Welcome to church planting.

Early Days

Two other couples made the move with us. One of the couples agreed to serve as our worship leaders. The husband played guitar and his wife was, in her words, a "chick drummer." The other couple was young with a capital Y. They had recently gotten married and were still, technically, teenagers. This young couple moved into our semifinished basement, which we called "an apartment." To be honest, we invited these guys into our lives because we feared that they wouldn't make it in their new marriage unless they had a couple to mentor them. And the husband was passionate about mercy ministry and cultural engagement, and we were short on staff.

We were all set for our new church. And to my astonishment, people began to come as I literally spent six to eight hours a day in the community engaging people relationally and telling them about the church when appropriate. Do you need evidence that God was involved in this? People came even though we were meeting in our basement, in a room one wall removed from the efficiency apartment and directly beneath our bedroom. I know a lot of churches start in basements, but our beginnings felt more than a little "cultish."

Eventually we escaped the basement and moved to a space at a local church that was declining in numbers and neighborhood impact.[11] This gracious congregation let us use their facility for free. Things were looking up, right? Hardly. One night after our core group meeting, my worship leader (with the chick drummer wife) called me on the phone.

"Bro, I can't do this anymore. I think I'm done," he said.

"Dude, it is OK; my wife can lead worship for a while and give you guys a break," I told him.

"No," he said. "I'm not talking about the church. I mean I don't think I can be married anymore; I'm done with my marriage."

He wasn't kidding. Within a few weeks he left his wife. A few months later, the young, former druggie and wannabe skater and current mercy ministry/cultural engagement guy decided that he didn't want to be married either. I spent hours with both of these men, pleading with them to fight for their marriages and love their wives. In the end, they both refused and divorced their wives.

Now, keep in mind that these were guys I knew. The worship leader and I had spent hours upon hours together. We probably spent twenty hours a week together for nine months, dreaming and planning and praying for this church, and I worked for him part-time installing ceramic tile. When he told me he was leaving his wife, I resigned from planting the church, unofficially.

I went home to Amie, who was pregnant with our second child, and announced that I was quitting. "We can't quit," she

---

11. There is a great opportunity for partnership with struggling churches and new church plants. Read about this opportunity in my forthcoming book, *Replanter*, from Crossway.

said. "God has called us to do this!" I love my wife. She always seems to speak the truth at the right time. In this instance, her response shocked me, largely because she had spent the first six months crying about how she disliked the city, our house, and the fact that we had some more than slightly messed-up people living beneath our bedroom floor. Evidently, God had worked in her heart, and it was her courage and God's encouragement through her that kept me in the game.

For the next several months, we just kept pushing ahead. We held Bible studies and community events. We were desperately looking for a building in the urban core of our city, but couldn't find anything that worked. I approached several pastors about sharing space in their church facilities. I didn't find any space, but I did get some territorialism[12] and several rude remarks. Eventually, we secured a community center, basically a fancy YMCA, in a city-center area.[13] We called our church "The Journey." The community center called itself "The Center," and it happened to be located on Gay Avenue. We were The Journey meeting at The Center located on Gay Avenue. How anyone thought we were a cult is beyond me.

After a year of unofficially being a church, we officially launched The Journey in September of 2002 with thirty people. Though we grew slowly that first year, we had some interesting people visit us. One of those colorful characters was affectionately known as "Timmy the Pool Boy." Timmy worked for The Center, maintaining the indoor pools and hot tubs. Timmy was the first

---

12. I never understand territorialism from pastors. The latest numbers I've seen from Barna show that the number of unchurched adults has risen 92 percent between 1991 and 2004. In 1991, Barna estimated that there were 39 million unchurched American adults. By 2004, the number was 75 million. In my view, it will take a whole lot of different types and sizes of churches to reach those folks, so territorialism is working against the church rather than working with and for the church. For more information on statistics regarding the unchurched, please see www.barna.org/barna-update/article/5-barna-update/140-number-of-unchurched-adults-has-nearly-doubled-since-199.

13. The term "city-center" is often used to describe the geographical center of an urban area. It is often a place of affluence as opposed to the poverty of the inner city.

of many people we ministered to who had mental health issues. Timmy would answer rhetorical questions during my sermons, shout obscenities during worship, and burst into tears accompanied with loud sobbing during communion. Many times he would arrive early, generally when first-time visitors showed up, and entertain people by doing Tai Chi in the lobby of our makeshift worship space. While this was strange, it wasn't completely out of the ordinary at The Center, since many people would complete their workouts and join us for worship, glistening with sweat and carrying a less than fragrant aroma to offer the Lord during worship.

One Lord's Day, a Jewish lady came in after her workout and began to interrogate me. Now, I was used to talking to folks who were Jewish since upwards of 80,000 Jews reside in our city. But she was more hostile than any of my other Jewish friends. She informed me that she didn't like the fact that a Christian church was meeting in "her" community center and that she planned to get us thrown out because her husband was on the facility's Board of Directors. She was going on and on about the atrocities committed by the church throughout history when all of a sudden a book on our resources table caught her attention. The book was called *The Gospel according to Tony Soprano,* written by my friend Chris Seay.[14]

"Oooh, I love *The Sopranos,*" she said, her eyes sparkling with delight. I told her she could have a copy of the book, and she ceased her interrogation, grabbed the book, began reading immediately, and walked out of the room. Apparently, she never actually complained to her husband because we didn't get kicked out.

One Sunday during that first summer,[15] packed in the banquet room of our little community center/church, we held a child dedication. I remember that particular Sunday for two reasons. First, we are all sweating profusely because the air-conditioning

---

14. Chris Seay, *The Gospel according to Tony Soprano* (New York: Tarcher, 2002).

15. Church planters refer to the first summer after launch as "the dark night of the soul."

wasn't working. Second, one of the children being dedicated was the granddaughter of a deacon of Hanley Road Baptist Church, which was located just a few blocks down the street from where we were meeting.

After the service, the deacon approached me and suggested I meet the pastor of Hanley Road, who, he said, loved to help church plants. So, I went to meet Pastor Slade Johnston, expecting, quite honestly, to get the same old routine that I had experienced from other pastors who "loved to help church plants." But Pastor Slade was different.

First of all, he cared about theology and the ways theology informs how you do church. In the Reformed tradition to which Matt and I belong, theology informs not only preaching and church structure, but also helps maintain the church's outward focus in regard to evangelism. Pastor Slade and I were on the same page theologically and he was very interested in me, not just what our church might do to "their" building. At the end of our first meeting Pastor Slade asked when we met for worship.

"At 10:45," I said.

He mused, "Well, we meet then, but I'll tell you what. We'll move our service back to 9:00 a.m. so that you can have that time slot."

I was speechless, which is a big deal for me. But he wasn't done. "We also have a third floor in our education building that you can use for offices. And, we have a fellowship hall that can seat 150 people. Why don't you get your artists down there and make it cool?" he said.

After I picked my jaw up off the floor, I made him repeat himself as a way of pinching me to make sure I wasn't dreaming. He did, and soon thereafter we moved our offices, went to work on the fellowship hall, and relocated our worship service to Hanley Road on the one-year anniversary of our official launch.

We had just over a hundred adults when we began meeting at Hanley Road. What was cool is that on a weekend several groups used the building for worship. There was our church, Hanley Road Baptist, an Ethiopian church, and a Chinese church that shared the space throughout the week. We could have had a United Nations committee meeting in that building! Within a year we had doubled in attendance and had to start another service. Six months later we started a third service. Our church was growing.

Many of those attending considered themselves to be "spiritual" but not "religious." In other words, many of our attendees believed (or wanted to believe) in God but were skeptical or even opposed to church as they had known and experienced it. Those who came often remarked, "I love it that you're actually teaching from the Bible." What's interesting is that many of those people didn't believe the Bible ... yet. We also learned that what stood out to people was the context of challenging, biblical teaching in the context of a community of people who seemed to genuinely care for one another and spend time together.

We were now running 500 adults and realized we needed a bigger building—largely because we were committed to preaching the Bible, living together in community, and serving our community in practical ways that we will unpack later in the book.

I learned there was a local high school with a large auditorium that was available on Sundays for a reasonable monthly fee. What I wasn't told is that the auditorium was built in 1940s and hadn't been aesthetically enhanced since the Truman Administration. I know this because the oldest member of my church graduated in the late 1940s from that particular high school. But it was our best option at the time, so we moved our morning services to this huge, old, nasty auditorium with no air-conditioning, and tried to ignore the dinginess and the wide variety of four-letter words carved into the wooden theater-style seats. Because we had such a great relationship with Hanley Road and because it was near one of the universities we drew from, we kept a night service at that location. We accidentally became multisite before multisite was hip, cool, or trendy.

By this time I was beginning to realize that we might need to find a more permanent building situation. I had always assumed we would be a mobile church forever. Just about that time, the

Archdiocese of St. Louis decided to unload dozens of church buildings and properties all over the city. We were able to find one of these beautiful Catholic facilities, complete with a sanctuary, school building, rectory, and convent. In all, we got nearly 60,000 square feet of space for a reasonable price in the heart of the south side of our great and broken city. We left the "cozy confines" of Maplewood High and moved into the former Holy Innocents Catholic Church in June of 2006. That summer we also encouraged twenty of our members who lived in a far western suburb to go with our first church planting intern, Trey Herweck, to plant Refuge Church.[16]

We continued our night service at Hanley Road and began to think about how we could best reach people driving into our services from the western suburbs. Our elders were bothered by the fact that it was taking over thirty minutes for over a hundred of our members to get to church.

We knew as well that though they were willing to make the drive, the likelihood of their non-Christians friends making such a drive was low. In addition, we were beginning to sense that the best situation was for people who attended our campuses to actually live in the neighborhood. With all these suburbanites' driving into our city campus, we found that our strategy of reaching the neighborhood wasn't working as well as we'd hoped. People from outside of the neighborhood were taking up seats that could be occupied by people from inside the neighborhood. So, we gathered seventy-five of the people who were driving into the city and began a campus in their area eight months after we moved into our new building.

Much has happened since that time. We've experienced criticism from the left and from the right. More "free-thinking" Christians and non-Christians have criticized us for our stance on the authority of Scripture, male eldership, and a variety of other hot-button issues. We've also been roundly criticized from the right by fellow evangelicals who think we are too "loose" in our

---

16. www.seekrefuge.net.

cultural engagement. This particular "rift" was highlighted when The Journey became a blip on the national news radar because of a front page article the *St. Louis Post-Dispatch* ran about an outreach ministry we hosted out of a local brew house.[17]

As we have weathered the storms of controversy, we've tried to stay focused on the gospel and our mission to take the gospel into the St. Louis metro area and beyond. In the fall of 2008 we launched our fourth campus across the Mississippi River in neighboring Illinois, and also spun off another self-sustaining ministry designed to reach and serve the artists of St. Louis.[18]

In 2010, we launched our fifth campus, which started because of the heart of a member of our church who owned a thrift store and desired a place for people who frequented there to go to church. The Journey is seeking to be a gospel-centered, missional church in that particular area of our state, and the indigenous leadership that developed there has done an excellent job of living out the gospel in their unique context.

God has been good to our church. As I have reflected on the stories and people that make up our history, I am reminded that through the struggles and joys, the tears and cheers, God has been present in it all. We have seen over sixty interns go through our intern program and serve God all over the world. We have planted six autonomous churches with our staff, elders, money, and buildings.

By God's grace we will continue to share the gospel. And we will continue to seek creative ways to share it with the culture around us, even as God uses the gospel to redeem lives and sharpen our own character. We serve him as missionaries, dispatched in his service.

---

17. The original article is no longer available in the *Post-Dispatch*'s online archives, but an article in *Christianity Today* is available at www.christianitytoday.com/ct/2007/july/6.16.html. A Google search on "Journey Beer Bible" will give you plenty of quality reading as well.

18. www.theluminaryarts.com.

CHAPTER 3

Engaging Austin: Academics, Activists, and Artists (Matt)

I (Matt) grew up in a Christian home with parents who loved God. Of course they wanted to make sure I did too, so from my earliest days I was at church every Sunday, week after week. Being raised in the church "paid off" eventually, and when I was eight years old I had a *true* conversion experience. I say "true" because I know that many kids may profess faith at a young age without really understanding what it means to be saved—or even who it is that is saving them! Certainly there were many unanswered questions and gaps in my knowledge, but I believed the gospel and I trusted in Jesus.

Still, even though I had trusted in Jesus, during my middle school and high school years I often rebelled against the authorities in my life. By God's grace, I somehow avoided many of the activities and habits that could have sent me off the deep end; and after graduating from high school, I made the decision to attend Texas A&M University in College Station, Texas.

It was during that first year away from home that I first realized that something was wrong in my life. Even though I had trusted Jesus as my Savior and faithfully believed that he was the forgiver of my sins and my only hope for eternal life, I really hadn't *surrendered* my life to him. I trusted God's promise in the gospel, but I wasn't living as if Jesus was my Lord, giving him free reign in my life to do whatever he willed whenever he wished. As a freshman in college, I sensed God stirring in my heart once again, this time calling me to dedicate my *entire* life to him. I asked him to take all of me—my gifts, talents, time, money, brain, and body—and do with them as he pleased. And God responded to my prayers by claiming me for his work and ministry.

He called me to be a pastor.

Fast-forward three years now, to my junior year of college. One of my college buddies was in the Texas A&M Corps of Cadets,[1] and I was attending his bachelor party in Austin that evening. Now I had never been to Austin before, but because I was an Aggie,[2] I knew that I didn't like Austin and would never like Austin. In case you are wondering *why* I dislike Austin (I'm guessing you aren't from Texas), Austin is the home of the University of Texas. And there is a long, storied, and *intense* rivalry between the Texas Longhorns of UT-Austin and the Texas A&M Aggies. For my entire life I had been trained to dislike the Longhorns, and since all Longhorns come from Austin, I naturally disliked Austin.

My first Austin experience began at Austin's famed Sixth Street. Known for its bars and clubs and for the legendary musicians who made those bars and clubs famous,[3] Sixth Street is Austin's equivalent of the French Quarter in New Orleans or Times Square in Manhattan. In other words, if you are in Austin and want to have fun and/or get into potentially life-altering trouble, you head straight for Sixth Street.

After the two-and-a-half-hour drive from College Station, my friends and I parked along Sixth Street and got out of the car to stretch our legs. For reasons that will never be known, a guy we had never met or seen before suddenly pulled his car next to ours, stuck a semiautomatic pistol out the window, and shot at us! The bullet struck yards away from where we were standing, and though no one was hurt, we all needed a fresh set of undergarments after the Austin equivalent of a welcome basket.

---

1. The Corps of Cadets at Texas A&M is the oldest student group on campus and is what one might call a "big deal" at A&M.

2. "Aggie" is a nickname for students at land-grant and agricultural colleges like A&M. Embracing the agricultural heritage in its fullness, "Aggie" is the nickname of A&M sports teams as well as students.

3. Greats like Willie Nelson, Stevie Ray Vaughn, Robert Earl Keen, and Jerry Jeff Walker played at bars and clubs up and down Sixth Street.

I had been in Austin for three minutes and had already been shot at!

Despite our near-death experience/greeting, we had a great time at our friend's bachelor party. Following the festivities, my friends and I headed back toward our car, which meant walking right through the crazy, colorful, eclectic mash of students, drunks, tourists, revelers, and homeless people on Sixth Street.

One of my friends, an Aggie football player, was in our crew, and from the dark recesses of a Sixth Street alley, a homeless man stepped toward us and punched my football playing friend right in the face. And this was no rabbit punch; this was a full-blown haymaker that sent my buddy straight to the ground, blood pouring from his nose and mouth. Before a street fight could break out, a police officer who had seen the whole thing intervened and arrested the second member of the Austin Welcoming Committee to greet us.

It was my inaugural trip to the capital of Texas. I had been in Austin for three hours, and I'd been shot at *and* involved in a street fight. Now I *really* didn't like Austin.

Austin — The Greatest City to Live In

Despite my initial dislike for Austin, my opinion of the city was far from the norm. In fact, most people who come to Austin and live in the city just *love* it. Austin exerts a peculiar hold on the American imagination. The city consistently ranks among the best cities to live in. According to various surveys, Austin is the number one city for jobs, green/environmental concerns, growing businesses, and economic vitality.[4] Richard Florida, a social scientist who researches the "creative class" and profiles cities where the creative class enjoys particular influence, says Austin citizens report high satisfaction levels across all of the categories

---

4. Rankings compiled from published reports by Rosalind Hejl. Located at www.weloveaustin.com/aboutaustin/comp_austin.html, accessed on July 10, 2009. Also, According to *Money Magazine*, Austin rated the second-best city to live in the United States in 2006.

surveyed.[5] Austinites are among the happiest people in the nation when asked about the quality of life in their city.

Why do people love Austin? For one, there are jobs and continued economic prosperity. With the exception of a few recession years, Austin's economy keeps growing steadily. Even in 2009, during the worst economic downturn in the United States since the Great Depression, Austin's economy continued to thrive.

Intellectual life pulsates in this town with four universities, a community college, and two seminaries. You can't overestimate the influence of the sprawling University of Texas, with its 37,000 undergrads and 2,500 faculty members. When most of a town's waiters and waitresses seem to have PhDs, it's safe to say that this town is an intellectual's kind of town. UT professors from all kinds of disciplines regularly win scholarly awards, earn patent discoveries, and publish important books and journal articles. All this contributes to the constant flow of ideas that characterizes Austin's culture.

On the arts and entertainment scene, Austin hosts a massive music, film, and arts festival called "South by Southwest." More than a thousand artists play their music or screen their films at "South By," which takes over Austin's urban core every March. In the fall, we do it all over again with the Austin City Limits Festival.

Another reason people love Austin is the availability of outdoor activities and the rugged beauty of the landscape. Austin sits on the foothills to Texas hill country, ringed by three man-made lakes. These hills and waterways provide seemingly infinite opportunities for outdoor recreation.

Austin also possesses a fondness for local community. Do people in other cities care about buying local products and fostering community? Of course. But in Austin, people are disturbingly passionate about keeping things local. Austinites work hard to keep big box stores out of the city's central core, and they intentionally patronize locally owned stores. Locals possess a fierce passion to

---

5. Richard Florida, *Who's Your City: How the Creative Economy Is Making Where to Live the Most Important Decision of Your Life* (New York: Basic Books, 2008), 155.

keep out the "sameness" they perceive in national retail stores. People in Austin buy books, coffee, ice cream—everything they can—from local stores.

Austinites love Austin because they intentionally cultivate a tolerance and a love for the different kinds of people and varied interests in this town. One group of Austinites even started a campaign called "Keep Austin Weird," which is a nod to the funky, diverse, tolerant, neighborly culture here. In a place where hippies, musicians, financiers, software programmers, and cattlemen mingle with ease, Austin is a sometimes mellow, sometimes boisterous community that attracts people from all over the world.

And despite getting shot at and punched at within the first few hours of arriving, I now love Austin too.

To Plant or Not to Plant?

Given this introduction to the city in which I now pastor, you are probably asking: How did I decide to plant a church in Austin? The answer is "a calling."

After graduating from college I worked in youth ministry for a few years before a biblical, faithful Methodist church in The Woodlands, Texas, called me as their associate pastor. It was here that I met and worked alongside one of the most gifted worship leaders I've ever known, seen, or heard, named Chris Tomlin. My role as associate pastor gave me an opportunity to preach more than I had ever preached, and I realized that effective communication of the Bible is a gift God has given me. The more I preached, the more I began to see spiritual fruit born in people's lives. I saw the Spirit transform people's lives as I communicated. In 1 Corinthians Paul writes that there's a specific way in which the Spirit of God manifests himself through all Christians, and I was seeing this happen in me when I exercised the gift of preaching and teaching.

The more I reflected on what God was doing in and through me, the more I discerned God calling me to be a pastor. I realized I had a couple of choices: I could assume the pastorate of an existing church, or I could start one. I didn't know anything about starting a new church except that it was a crazy endeavor, statistically destined for failure, and was sure to be the hardest thing I could ever choose to do.

So, for a couple of years I simply prayed about what God seemed to be stirring in me. I asked God to make my calling clear. My prayer was, "God, you're going to have to *speak* to me and tell me if this is something you really want me to do. You're going to have to make it clear."

Church Planting Class at Southwestern

At the time I was asking God for clarity about whether or not to plant a church, I was also completing a Master of Divinity degree at Southwestern Baptist Theological Seminary (SWBTS). As part of the degree program I took a week-long intensive elective course on church planting. At the beginning of the class the professor tested every student's aptitude for planting a church. Where applicable, the test was also given to a student's spouse. The assessment took four hours and consisted of 400 to 500 questions. The assessors used a one-to-five scale in each category, with five being the highest score.

My wife, Jen, and I only scored one five on the entire test, which we garnered was based on *her* ability to plant a church! While this was not the most heartening result I could have received, the good news was still good. According to the assessor we had done very well. Our scores landed us in the top 1 percent of the nation in terms of our likelihood to plant a successful church in a healthy way. As I reflected on the results of the assessment, I thought, "God, after two years of prayer for clarity, this seems like something of a green light. Thank you!"

Following our assessment, my church planting professor approached me about planting with the seminary's church panting initiative called the Nehemiah Project.[6] He asked me where I was currently serving in ministry.

---

6. See www.swbts.edu/index.cfm?pageid=629 for more information on the Nehemiah Project.

Before I go any further, you need to understand a few details I haven't shared with you. For one, I'm a Baptist. More than that, I'm a Southern Baptist. I grew up in a Southern Baptist church. My parents and grandparents were Southern Baptists. So here I was, a dyed-in-the-wool Southern Baptist, conversing with a Southern Baptist professor at a Southern Baptist seminary about my current ministry setting.

"Actually," I replied, "I'm an associate pastor at the Woodlands United Methodist Church."

The next several seconds felt like one of those scenes in an old Western movie when a six-shooter toting outlaw bent on revenge walks into a saloon, the music from the player piano stops, and the focus of the whole bar shifts to the new cowboy.

"You work *where*?"

I repeated, "A Methodist church."

"Why?" he asked, dumbfounded.

In an attempt to dial back the increasing awkwardness of the conversation, I played the Chris Tomlin card.

"Have you ever heard of Chris Tomlin?"

"No," said the professor.

Okay, that didn't help.

As our conversation continued, it became clear that it didn't matter that I was serving at an evangelical Methodist church. It didn't matter that I was enrolled at the same seminary where this man taught. It didn't even matter that I'd passed the assessment administered by Southern Baptists for the purpose of planting Southern Baptist churches. Ultimately, my professor informed me that the seminary would not support my church planting efforts because I was currently serving at a Methodist church. What I'd hoped would be a dynamic, fruitful partnership with the seminary and the Nehemiah Project was not to be.

The Interview That Changed Everything

The final exam for my church planting class was to interview one of twenty-five church planters in the Dallas/Fort Worth area, and then write a twenty-five page paper on the interview. The professor tasked us with reflecting upon and writing about the planter's ministry philosophy, mistakes, and successes. Since the drive from the seminary to The Woodlands is a good three-and-a-half hours, the idea of returning to the Metroplex area to do an interview— seven hours round-trip—struck me as something I'd like to avoid. Because of this, my primary criterion for picking out a planter from among the twenty-five listed was simply this: which pastor required the least amount of driving to reach?

On a whim, I called the church I had picked on a Friday around noon to see if there was *any* chance I could get a meeting with the pastor on my way home for the weekend. I got hold of his assistant and surprisingly, the pastor had just had a meeting cancel.

The pastor led a church that was growing rapidly and they already had a thousand people attending each Sunday. He had already walked the path I was looking to walk, and the church he served had become established. We talked for an hour and a half, connecting at a deep level as he shared his successes ... and his failures. Near the end of our time, I shared with him a bit about the highs and lows of the past week—that we had assessed well for planting, but the fact that I was working at a Methodist church had closed doors with the seminary. I admitted how the rejection from the Nehemiah Project had crushed me and left me wondering what was next. It felt as if God had answered two years of prayers, and then, abruptly pulled the rug out from under me.

This man looked at me thoughtfully for a moment and said, "Well, Matt, you've just been talking to the wrong people. I'm the head recruiter for the Southern Baptist Convention of Texas Church Planting organization. When do you want to get started?"

I looked at him, a bit confused, "What are you talking about? I just met you."

He said, "I've been around a lot of church planters and I can just tell when God's moving."

"But I work at a Methodist church," I said.

"I don't care," he said. "When do you want to get started?"

That conversation reopened the door for me and began a

church planting project with the Southern Baptists in Texas. I immediately called my wife.

"Jen, you know how we've been praying for two years about starting a church?"

"Yes."

Laughing, I shared the good news with her. "Well, we're doing it. So start praying *harder*!"

Chris Tomlin's Idea

The next night I had dinner with the youth pastor of our church and our worship leader, Chris Tomlin, and shared with them what I felt God was calling me to do. Chris's career was just starting to take off, and the spotlight of national fame and attention was starting to shine on him. While many people think Chris's greatest gift is writing songs, it's not. His real gift is leading others in worship. Not many people can stand before a crowd of human beings and lead the entire person — heart, soul, and body — in such passionate, God-honoring worship.

At dinner I told Chris what had happened, "I've got some good news and some sad news. I'm going to be leaving the The Woodlands Methodist Church. I'm leaving to plant a church somewhere in the state of Texas."

Chris didn't say much at that point, other than a heartfelt, "We're going to miss you." The next morning was Sunday. I walked into the sanctuary ten minutes before the service and Chris walked up to me, and he put his hand on my shoulders. He said, "Matt, I couldn't sleep. I've been thinking about this all night long. I want to go with you. I want to go with you ... and I want to go to Austin."

Chris Tomlin? Austin? This was a complete shock to me. For one thing, I was shocked that Chris would want to join me on this adventure. The Lord was raising Chris to such a level of prominence and influence that it hadn't occurred to me that he would want to start from scratch and plant a church. Second, as I shared before, I'm a Texas Aggie (Texas A&M) — and not merely any Aggie, but part of the Corp of Cadets at A&M—the full-throated, tradition-revering, crazy-passionate core of all that is A&M. My entire family went to A&M. And from the time I was a little kid I was trained not to like the University of Texas. To have any regard whatsoever for anything UT was borderline heresy and sin. In my circles you root for two teams: the Aggies and whoever is playing against UT.

Since Austin is the home of the University of Texas, I knew it wasn't an option for me, so I said to Chris, "First, I would *love* for you to come with me to plant a church. But there is *no way* in the world I'm going to Austin, Texas. So forget about that."

We began to travel all over the state looking for a place to plant a church. We looked at Houston, Ft. Worth, various suburbs of Dallas. I even looked at Granbury, which is a small town about an hour southwest of Ft. Worth. But Chris simply couldn't get away from the idea of Austin. No matter where we looked, Chris kept coming back to Austin. Then, God began to work in my heart, saying: "I've called you to plant a church and reach people who don't know me, and Austin is one of the *most* unreached cities in the nation."

A Church for the City

Like most church planters, I assumed that we'd find a nice place to get started in the suburbs. That's where the real estate development is, the young single adults and young families; that's where the energy is, the money, the action; and frankly, that's where most church plants decide to set up shop.

But in the back of my mind, I had a lingering doubt about that strategic decision. Something a professor said in a seminary class was like a burr in my saddle. He said, "I find it interesting that the Holy Spirit continues to 'lead' young church planters to rich white suburban areas." His comment provoked me enough to remain open to considering a plant in the urban center of Austin.

Then, as we were praying and looking for a place to plant, Chris made a statement that cemented our commitment to the city. He said, "If you want to reach a city, you have to go to the *heart* of the city." I knew Chris was right. The *cultural* center of Austin lay not in the vast areas of tract housing and strip malls springing up on the ever-extended periphery; rather, the spirit of Austin, the life of the city, was animated by the central core. That's where the Capitol and University were; that's where the financial center and entertainment centers were. In other words, the urban core of Austin is where culture was made, and it was home to almost 300,000 unreached people.

Thus, the Lord led us to abandon our initial dream of a suburban plant and move to the heart of the city. In many ways, like Jonah, God compelled me to go against my natural inclinations, my training, and my background, to plant in the heart of Austin. I was a conservative, small-town, hard-core Aggie used to ministering in comfortable and financially affluent suburbs. Yet the Lord led me to plant a church in a context that was almost the complete opposite of who I was.

Doing Our Part to Keep Austin Weird

On December 2, 2002, the first night that we launched The Stone, I was driving in the South Congress neighborhood to our newly rented facility, and I almost drove off the road when I saw a man walking down the street wearing nothing but a thong and ballet shoes. This was my first encounter with the legendary Leslie, one of the quintessential local characters of Austin. Incidentally, shortly after that night, Leslie announced his candidacy for mayor of Austin.

He came in third.

Leslie and the tens of thousands of other Austin residents certainly do their part to keep Austin weird. I know that God loves them, and I am grateful that he gives me a heart and opportunity to love them as well. I experience deep joy in loving and serving the people in our community, no matter how weird they may be. And the beautiful truth is that our church, in its own way, is helping to keep Austin weird. Through our songs and our preaching, we are seeking to manifest the presence of Jesus in this community. Now, that's weird, if you really stop to think about it!

Jesus to the Fore

We quickly outgrew the junior high school where we were meeting and moved to the Stephen F. Austin High School, named for the "Father of Texas" who founded the original colony for American settlers (with Mexican permission) in the early nineteenth century.

From the beginning I had determined, by God's grace and with all the labor, passion, and intensity that I could summon, that I would introduce the people who came to worship at The Stone to Jesus. Jesus is who we are really all about. We exist to magnify him, to proclaim him, and to follow him. To make sure we were all on same page, guided by the same vision and mission, I taught through the gospel of John for the first four years, unpacking the stories and teachings of our King to people who barely knew him ... and some who didn't know him at all.

We pushed Jesus to the fore of all we did.

God birthed in our midst an increasing desire to live as people on mission. At around this time, the term *missional* was beginning to become something of a "buzz" word. Though some of the concepts associated with the word missional have lost their clarity because of the variety of different meanings attached to it now, the concept for us in those early years was simple. Jesus made it clear that the gospel was to be preached to all the nations and then the end would come. We knew that we had a job to do. We have about thirty years, give or take a few, to make our mark on church history. Thirty years to make a dent in our city and reach the nations. And then our time is over, and we pass the torch on to the next generation.

So, through the course of several years we talked a lot about being a person on mission and collectively about what it meant to be the body of Christ on mission together. We constantly challenged our people to think outside themselves, to be dissatisfied merely sitting in their chairs gathering knowledge. We called the people of The Stone to take the great truths they were learning about Jesus in Scripture and put them into practice at work, in their dorms, in their apartments, and inside and outside the classroom. Our emphasis was on no longer just learning, but also *doing*, being a part of the redemption of other people's lives, as God's Spirit enabled us. As the Lord changed us through this process, being "on mission" became part of our DNA—our core identity as a church.

What God Showed Me on Sabbatical

As we continued to grow and mature as a body, a major change occurred in 2006 while I was on a one-month sabbatical. A man in our church paid for my wife and me to stay at St. Johns in the Virgin Islands in a rented cabin on the side of a mountain overlooking Chocolate Hole Bay. It was a scene of absolute beauty.

Every morning I'd grab a cup of coffee and my Bible and journal, and I'd go study for a few hours. I *love* studying God's Word, and having uninterrupted time in such a beautiful place to study was a great gift. I wanted to study the Old Testament all the way through for a couple of weeks, and as I read through the Old Testament I began to notice a theme. As God pursued the people of Israel, as they acted out certain behaviors and tendencies of their heart contrary to his Word, the Lord would warn them. He would call his people out of their behaviors, and if they persisted in their behavior, he would warn them again and again. But if they resolutely persisted in their defiance of the Lord, he would eventually remove his blessing from them.

I detected three patterns of disobedience in the Israelites. First, the Israelites would turn to other gods and worship idols. I read God's reaction to the Israelites chasing other gods, and it was the reaction of pain and hurt. Whoring after other gods wounded him. Repeatedly, God told them that the worship of false gods was, to him, similar to a wife cheating on her husband. Second, I detected a pattern of a general lack of holiness. Even when they weren't actively following other gods, the Israelites often failed to make use of the means that God had provided for them to grow in their relationship with him. They were easily ensnared by their own sinful desires. Finally, I saw a pattern among the Israelites as they neglected caring for the poor. God consistently warned them that their lack of concern for the poor indicated a lack of love in their hearts.

As I was reading, God struck me afresh with a passage in Amos 5:21. God says to his people, "I hate, I despise your feasts." The nuance of the Hebrew word here is similar to the idea of "draining." In other words, God was saying that when the Israelites got together for their religious festivals, their actions would *drain* him. Rather than increasing his glory and joy in their worship, the festivals decreased his delight in the praise of his people.

The Lord goes on in that same passage to say, "I take no delight in your solemn assemblies." Literally, the Hebrew word for "delight" has the nuance of "likes to smell." In some sense, God is telling the Israelites, "Your solemn assemblies, when you gather in my name, stink. Even though you are offering burnt offerings and grain offerings to me, they have a bad odor. Get rid of the noise of your songs." There was something that the Israelites were doing that made their worship stink in God's nostrils. Their worship music had become nothing more than white noise to the Lord.

As I read these passages, that verse stopped me in my tracks. What in the world were these people doing wrong that would lead God, who is *jealous* for our worship, to tell them to "shut up!"? What was causing their worship gatherings to literally "stink"? I began to drill down and study what the Israelites were doing ... and not doing. Looking back to Amos 5, God shares about how the Israelites were imposing heavy rent on the poor in their midst (5:11). Then, in verse 12 God talks about how their transgressions and sins were great—because they distressed the poor and turned aside the poor at the city gates! Looking back to the previous chapter, I noticed that the Lord calls the women of Israel "cows of Bashan" (4:1). The cows of Bashan were prized cattle, known for their beauty and fatness, and the Lord calls these Israelite women cows because they oppressed the poor and crushed the needy. God had blessed them and they had become fat and lazy in their blessing, but they were not living to bless others.

The Holy Spirit flooded me with conviction. In a raw, desperate moment, I asked the Lord, "Has Austin Stone become this?"

We were growing like crazy at the time, and the Lord had blessed us with abundant financial resources. When we worked through our budget process, the Lord often brought in hundreds of thousands of dollars more than we had budgeted. We were on mission, and we were giving money to missions, but I knew in that moment that regardless of our programs and our donations of money to missions, we could still be selfish, self-centered people, caring only for ourselves. And if that was true, maybe our worship had also become something that God despised. Were we becoming fat, failing to bless others? Were we like the Israelites turning aside the poor at the gate?

While I was on my sabbatical, we were in the midst of looking for some land where we could build a permanent church facility. We had looked at a fast-growing, hip, young professional area of town known as the Arboretum, as well as several other locations all over city. But there was one part of town called the St. Johns neighborhood that was under-resourced, impoverished, and withering under the highest crime rate in the city. In a raw, deeply vulnerable moment with the Lord I prayed, "If you want me to take this church into St. Johns, I'll do it."

That was a difficult prayer for me. It was difficult even for the words to come out of my mouth. It was a prayer of surrender, saying, "Lord, I give up my worldly ambitions of what kind of church we're supposed to be. Austin Stone is your church. *We* are your church. I want your church to be whatever you want it to look like."

Even though I was on my sabbatical and not to be interrupted, I received a call three days later from the real estate agent who was helping us locate a property for our permanent facility. Cautiously, he let me know that he had found something, "Matt, I've got some land, but I don't think you're going to like it." He described the potential land, and let me know that there were so many crack pipes, needles, condoms, and smashed liquor bottles scattered on the ground that you'd be afraid to even walk on it. But it was fifteen acres ... right in the center of the city.

I remembered my prayer just a few days earlier, and simply said, "I think we're supposed to buy it." And that was how Austin Stone changed. We became a church in and for the city, a church that was about to learn what it meant to *love* the city.

Part 2

IN AND
FOR THE
CITY

CHAPTER 4

Contextualization (Darrin)

Pastors Can Be Idiots Too

Prior to the official launch of The Journey, we held Bible studies and missional events to encourage our launch team and to draw in non-Christians interested in learning more about our community. One of the most memorable of these "missional events" was the time when I (Darrin) decided it would be wise to gather all the men of the church in the basement of my home for a marathon viewing of the Emmy-worthy MTV "variety show," *Jackass*. We sent out a general invitation to the community, and the response was overwhelmingly positive. Nothing attracts a bunch of dudes to a basement like the opportunity to watch a group of irreverent grown men prolong their adolescence by acting like middle schoolers, all on national television.

If you aren't familiar with *Jackass*, I can sum it up for you in a phrase: "Don't try this at home!" Which is another way of saying, "Many young men are morons and are more than willing to prove it in front of a camera and an audience for not much money." Known for its objectionable humor and its dangerous homemade stunts, *Jackass* provided an odd gathering tool for a start-up church. But when young men who embodied my target demographic started showing up and engaging in conversation, I felt like a cutting-edge hipster who happened to be a pastor. This was, in my mind, confirmation of my down-to-earth personality and general awesomeness, and I was convinced that I was the best pastor without an official church in town. This über-missional event would be the beginning of conquering St. Louis for the gospel by means of shrewd cultural engagement. The night was young and the sky was the limit for ministry victory.

And then the wheels came off the church bus.

This missional shindig was a raging success for all of ten minutes. Everything changed when our least-churched guy brought several bottles of hard liquor and began encouraging many of our non-Christians and new Christians to drink shots of liquid Christian liberty in Jesus' name. Before I knew what was happening, the party lost every bit of gospel focus and devolved into something worthy of an MTV show of its own: Church Plant Gone Wild!

I didn't know exactly how to respond to the billowing chaos, so I avoided/justified it by having one-on-one conversations with some of the non-Christian dudes whose tongues were being chemically loosened by the booze. But in my mind, I knew something had gone terribly wrong.

We'll return to this story in a bit and look at just what went wrong with my approach, but first, let's take a look at one of Matt's finer pastoral moments as well.

Pastors Say the Darndest Things

In October of 2009, Matt was leading his church through a study of the book of Genesis, which as of this printing is still ongoing, though there have been some minor sermon detours along the way for holidays and special occasions. In his first sermon of the Genesis series, Matt spent some time discussing Genesis 1:1 and the declaration of God as creator recorded therein.[1]

Now, as a pastor, you cannot tackle a book like Genesis and texts like Genesis 1 and 2 and not deal with creation. More specifically, you cannot preach on these texts for a modern audience and avoid discussing evolution. While Matt did an admirable job explaining that Genesis 1 was not written as a response to the

---

1. You can listen to audio of Matt's sermon "In the Beginning Was Jesus" from October 18, 2009, by visiting www.austinstone.org/resources/sermons/month/2009/10/.

theory of evolution because there was no such thing as the theory of evolution in the ancient world, he did what any pastor ought to do and acknowledged the elephant in the room. He took a few minutes to explain his personal opinion about God as creator and the theory of evolution.

Now I know Matt well, and I have heard him preach many times. He is a careful expositor of Scripture and a thoughtful and passionate preacher. Unfortunately, on this particular Sunday Matt ventured off his prepared notes at this point and made a couple of jokes and disparaging comments, remarks that made the theory of evolution sound like it came from the comic strips. After stating his personal position on the matter and asking a few thought-provoking questions, he moved on with the rest of the sermon.

Unwittingly, though, his sermon strategy had just alienated hundreds of people sitting there in the room with him, from the University of Texas students studying the natural sciences to the University of Texas professors *teaching* those students in the natural sciences. In a matter of mere minutes, Matt had made the entire life work of many of the scientists in his audience seem like a complete waste of time. And for many in the congregation who were studying the matter carefully and thoughtfully, Matt had basically communicated that they'd be better served by studying underwater basket weaving than dealing with all that "monkey business."

To make matters even worse, he later learned that an Austin Stone member who happened to be a University of Texas faculty member in the natural sciences had chosen that day to bring a non-Christian colleague to the service. This colleague had recently expressed an interest in the gospel and was excited to hear what Matt had to say about the creation account in Genesis. This church member made sure that Matt knew that his non-Christian friend no longer had any interest in returning to the Stone because he felt ridiculed. Clearly, his beliefs and professional pursuits made him unwelcome at their church.

Now keep both of these stories in your mind for a few more moments. We'll return to them soon and detail exactly what went wrong in each situation, showing you why these are both examples of *ineffective* ministry.

What Is Contextualization?

Before we go any further, we need to define the word that makes up this chapter's title and focus: *contextualization*. When I use this word, I am referring to the particular way in which we as Christians communicate the gospel. The word *contextualization* basically means to consider the *context*—the setting and the culture—into which you are communicating your message and, if necessary, consider how you should adjust your message (without *changing* it) so that those to whom you are speaking are more likely to hear and accurately understand what you are saying to them. Tim Keller offers this simple definition: "Contextualization is adapting my communication of the gospel without changing [the gospel's] essential character."[2]

I would suggest that the key phrase to keep in mind in Keller's definition is that last part—"without changing [the gospel's] essential character." To allay any fears that contextualization involves selling out or changing an unchangeable message, it must be emphasized that contextualization is *not* an invitation to make the gospel say whatever you might want it to say. Contextualization does *not* give us permission to drop the offensive parts of the gospel and avoid biblical topics like sin and hell. Contextualization is *not* ultimately even about the *content* of the gospel. It's primarily about *the way you communicate* the unchanging content of the gospel.

Healthy contextualization, therefore, demands that the gospel be preached in a language people know, with concepts, images, and metaphors that are faithful to Scripture and understandable to people. This process is more of an art than a science, as Dean Flemming notes. "Contextualization is the dynamic and compre-

---

2. Tim Keller, "Context Sensitive," www.redeemer2.com/themovement/issues/2004/feb/advancingthegospel_3.html.

hensive process by which the gospel is incarnated within a concrete historical or cultural situation."[3]

As I (Darrin) wrote in my book *Church Planter*, "[Flemming's] definition demonstrates the kind of flexibility needed to appropriately contextualize. Adapting gospel ministry into a culture requires nimbleness, pliability, and creativity. A good preacher, for example, must be able to exegete not only the text, but also the culture of the hearers in order to be a faithful and fruitful missionary. We are to bring the gospel through the church to the world and avoid allowing the world to influence the church and corrupt the gospel."[4]

The key to ministry in any and every context, both now and for the last two thousand years, is missionary flexibility. To reach a culture, a good missionary will adapt gospel communication and ministry to that culture. In other words, good missionaries must learn to translate the gospel for the particular context in which they are called to proclaim it.[5] Contextualization means that we communicate *with* a culture's terms but not *on* the culture's terms.[6] Those involved in ministry for a city must communicate in a way that is understandable to those who reside in the city. This communication must be more than just our verbal proclamation, what we say through our preaching and teaching. It includes our leadership structure, our written communication, and even the aesthetics of our facility. "Everything preaches," someone has said, "but not everything reaches." The question is not only, "Is my topic a good one to preach?" but, "Does anyone understand the message I'm preaching?"

That is the concern of contextualization, and the basic question we are examining here is: How do we make the unchanging gospel

---

3. Dean Flemming, *Contextualization in the New Testament: Patterns for Theology and Mission* (Downers Grove, IL: InterVarsity Press, 2005), 19.

4. Darrin Patrick, *Church Planter: The Man, the Message, and the Mission* (Wheaton, IL: Crossway, 2010), 196.

5. To better understand the idea of translation, see Lamin Sanneh, *Translating the Message* (Maryknoll, NY: Orbis, 1989).

6. For a more thorough treatment of this concept, please read the chapter entitled "The How of Mission: Contextualization" in my book *Church Planter*.

comprehensible to people in an urban area, one that is changing daily? The tension we find in trying to contextualize the gospel message is challenging to navigate, but it is one that every good missionary and gospel-centered, missional church must step into at some point if they want to honor Christ's purpose for the church. The stories that we chose for the opening of this chapter illustrate this tension for us.

My story and Matt's story are different in several ways. My story is set in a weirdo basement party; Matt's story is set in a church. My story involves alcohol and bad TV; Matt's story involves teaching from the Bible.

But these stories are similar in one crucial way. Both stories result from the same failure, a failure to appropriately contextualize the gospel for the people we were trying to reach. Matt and I failed to navigate thoughtfully the tension of gospel-centered contextualization.

My failure, unlike Matt's, was classic *over*-contextualization. Over-contextualization is when you view missional opportunities primarily through a cultural lens instead of a gospel lens. In this instance, I was more concerned with providing a cool, "unchurchy" environment than I was with making sure the environment didn't reflect poorly on the gospel. The guys I tried to reach needed healthy gospel boundaries around their newly discovered Christian liberty. I failed to provide that for them. I over-contextualized in my approach because I tried to make the gospel submit to the culture rather than letting my pop culture sensibilities submit to the gospel.

My esteemed coauthor, by contrast, was guilty of *under*-contextualization. Matt under-contextualized by failing to consider how he might communicate his thoughts in a way his audience would receive. Matt didn't take the time he should have to consider that there were several highly intellectual and influential professors in his audience with differing views about issues like the age of the earth. Some of these folks held legitimate, biblical positions that differed from Matt's conclusion; others may have held nonbiblical views, but they felt dismissed and insulted by Matt's offhand comments, which made it highly unlikely that they would respect-fully listen to Matt in his communication of the gospel message.

These stories of over- and under-contextualization provide an excellent springboard for us to consider yet another issue, closely related to contextualization: the importance of missionary flex-ibility for the advancement of the gospel. One of the greatest chal-lenges to reaching our cities with the gospel is finding ways of reaching the vast array of cultures that inhabit our cities. Andy Crouch writes about this urban multiculturalism in his insightful book *Culture Making*: "Multiculturalism begins with the simple observation that the cumulative, creative process of human cul-ture has happened in widely different places, with widely different results, throughout human history."[7] The melting pot of all these cultures is often most clearly visible in our cities.

What Are Cultures?

Many churches in our American context are trying to figure out how to do the admirable and necessary work of multiracial minis-try.[8] While we believe this is a good emphasis, increasingly in city contexts, churches must not only figure out how to reach different races within the same culture, but also different races from radi-cally differing cultures.[9]

This begs the question: What exactly are cultures? Again, Andy Crouch helps us: "Culture is, first of all, the name for our relentless,

---

7. Andy Crouch, *Culture Making: Recovering Our Creative Calling* (Downers Grove, IL: InterVarsity Press, 2008), 41.

8. See Mark DeYmaz, *Building a Healthy Multi-Ethnic Church* (San Francisco: Jossey-Bass, 2007).

9. We are not going into the vast challenges of race in the cities in this book because in all honesty, the Journey and the Stone are still trying to figure out the best ways to effectively address this difficult social issue. We are making headway, but we have a long way to go. For a good treatment of the theology of racial recon-ciliation and the role of the church, see Jarvis J. Williams, *One New Man: The Cross and Racial Reconciliation in Pauline Theology* (Nashville, TN: Broadman and Hol-man, 2010). Williams has a particularly interesting take on the differences between true racial reconciliation and simply striving for a diverse congregation.

restless human effort to take the world as it's given to us and make something else."[10] We, like the God who created us, are ourselves creators. We, as human beings in our own unique cultures, create out of those cultures. Because of the influence of our cultures, we humans select certain practices, symbols, and rituals and organize our lives around them, which enable us to make sense of the world. These practices, symbols, and rituals are the cumulative product of upbringing, environment, and the time we inhabit the earth.

Culture is really about what people think, how they feel, and what they do. For example, St. Louis is a city with people concerned about who's a native St. Louisan and who's not. One of the common jokes in St. Louis (funny because it's all too true) is that the first question you get asked in St. Louis is what school you went to. And they don't mean which college you attended. They mean which high school you attended. And what they really mean in asking the question in the first place is: Are you from around here? To be a part of St. Louis culture means that you are from St. Louis. So what happens when a nonnative St. Louisan can't answer the classic St. Louis question? Well, you feel like an idiot. You feel like you don't belong.

People from St. Louis want to know who's a native of the city because they want to associate them with some of the cultural values of the city. Typically, if you're from St. Louis, you are likely to value hard work, particularly if it is blue-collar, unionized work. You love the St. Louis Cardinals regardless of whether you love baseball or not. And if you drink beer, you drink Budweiser.

Obviously, these broad brush strokes can be used to paint a caricature of a St. Louisan, but there is something to all of this that we need to understand and consider as we think about the culture we are trying to reach. Somewhere in all of this, hidden within the caricatures and jokes, is a real piece of what St. Louis culture is all about.

When we speak about culture, we are describing this complex framework within which all of life is lived for a person or a group

---

10. Crouch, *Culture Making*, 23.

of people. Real life in an urban context isn't neatly segregated into distinct cultural communities. Instead, everyone is thrown together, living on top of one other, and there are endless cultures, subcultures, and tribes in any given city: "The culture of a people is its common attitude, style of living and thinking, rooted in its basic apprehension of reality."[11]

So, if it's true that culture consists of what people think, feel, and do, we need to get familiar with what the people in our cities think, feel, and do. And one way to move in this direction is to ask questions that help us unearth the real values that people have in order to communicate the gospel to them in a way they can understand. We can categorize these vital questions by considering their functions. There are questions that probe the mind, questions that uncover motivations, and questions that reveal methods. In other words, we need to be asking questions aimed at the head, the heart, and the hands of the people we want to reach and serve. Churches for their cities must ask questions of the head, heart, and hands because cultures are born from the head, hearts, and hands of people.

Head questions probe the thinking that people have regarding history, science, and education. They seek to understand how people process and understand truth: How did humans get here? Is history governed by a supreme being, or is it random and without purpose? Does science explain away God? Is there truth and can it be known?

Heart questions mine the core convictions that govern what people value: What do they suffer and sacrifice for? Where do they invest their time, talent, and treasure? What are people passionate about?

Hands questions look for the activities and events that people participate in: What do they do for entertainment? What do families do together? What events rally the community? How do they recreate? How are meals shared?

---

11. J. H. Bavinck, as quoted in Robert T. Coote and John Stott, *Down to Earth: Studies in Christianity and Culture* (Grand Rapids: Eerdmans, 1980), 148.

We listen to questions that people are asking, and we seek to give them God's answers in ways that they can understand.

Those who pursue healthy contextualization will not only ask questions of the culture, but will also listen to the questions that the culture is asking and respond to those questions with the gospel. This sounds like a nice, neat little formula for ministry success. Not so much. In reality, it is anything but nice, neat, and formulaic. This is due in large part to one of the primary challenges to contextualization: the Christian subculture. Churches tend to get so caught up in their own unique subculture—the Christian bubble—that they fail to incarnate their faith in the culture to which they've been called. In other words, churches can turn inward and get stuck. They lose their sense of mission and their ability to relate to the surrounding culture.

To help us more fully understand the complexity and value of healthy contextualization—and how we can avoid this inward focus—we will look to probably the best missiologist of the last half-century, Lesslie Newbigin.

Gospel, Church, Culture

Lesslie Newbigin was a British missionary who, armed with the gospel, went to India in the 1950s. His writings describe what he encountered in a cultures-laden country ignorant (for the most part) of Christianity. In order to bring the gospel to the culture through the church, he realized that several things needed to happen. First, preaching and worship needed to address non-Christians as well as Christians. That is, the corporate worship gathering had to be comprehensible to those who were unfamiliar with Christianity, its vocabulary, its rituals, and its beliefs.

Second, the members of the church had to see themselves as missionaries, people who were being sent by God with the gospel into the cultures they lived among and within.

Third, the church could not become so enamored with its own survival and maintenance that it forgot its mission. The church did not exist to simply serve itself; it existed to create a new community centered around the gospel.[12] Newbigin carefully listened to his culture and then tried to empower and equip the church, as it was being transformed by the gospel, to reach that culture.

Newbigin saw the church-making progress in his South India context, and his idea of *gospel movement* can assist us in thinking about our own cultural context. Toward that end, missiologist and Newbigin-devotee George Hunsberger has developed a diagram based on Newbigin's theology, outlining the relationships between the gospel, the church, and the culture.[13] What follows is a series of visual models based on Hunsberger's original diagram, models that can help us carefully avoid "unhealthy" contextualization. Let's first consider two "unhealthy" models of contextualization: syncretism and sectarianism.

The Dual Ditches

The call of God's people is to have an unwavering commitment to the gospel in the culture in which we live while maintaining our unique identity as the church of Jesus Christ. There are two ditches on either side of this narrow road that the church can fall into as it seeks to bring an unchanging gospel into our ever-changing culture.

Ditch 1: Syncretism

As is suggested by Figure 4.1, when the culture is prioritized over the gospel, you get what is commonly known as *syncretism*.

Syncretism occurs when the true Christian gospel is exchanged for a sterile gospel of relativism. In the syncretistic church the distinguishing attributes of the gospel are blended with the prevailing worldview, morality, and behaviors of the dominant culture so that Christianity loses its distinct voice in the culture it is trying

---

12. Lesslie Newbigin, *The Gospel in a Pluralist Society* (Grand Rapids: Eerdmans, 1989), is a must read for all pastors and leaders of gospel-centered missional churches.

13. George R. Hunsberger, *The Church between Gospel and Culture: The Emerging Mission in North America* (Grand Rapids: Eerdman, 1996), 9.

Syncretism
FIGURE 4.1

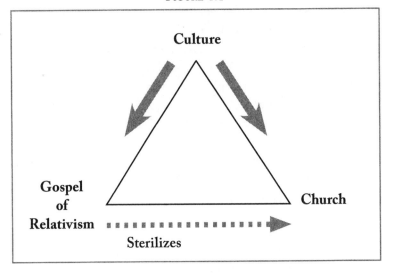

to influence and shape. Syncretism almost always begins with a good desire to be culturally relevant, but it always ends with a series of ever-changing cultural agendas that supplant the foundational truths of the Bible and the good news it heralds. This is why missiologist John Orme can accurately say that syncretism is "an odorless, tasteless gas, likened to carbon monoxide ... seeping into [the Christian] atmosphere."[14]

How can you recognize syncretism in the church landscape today? Consider the following scenario, which is generalized here as an illustration but is still increasingly common among many churches, even some churches that started out as good ol' Bible-believing evangelical churches.

Pastor Bill planted Love Church because of the burden he felt to answer this question: How can a church attract the people of this city and meet their needs in a practical way? The winsome pastor

---

14. John Orme, *The Paradox of Peace: Leaders, Decisions, and Conflict Resolution* (New York: Palgrave, 2004), 1, as cited in Gailynn Van Rheenen, "Contextualization and Syncretism," www.missiology.org/mrr/mmr38.pdf.

was a people-magnet and used his charisma to grow a launch team of 150 people. When Love Church officially opened its doors to the city, 300 people showed up. Today, just two years later, Love Church hosts an average of 1,000 people every weekend.

From the outside, Pastor Bill is considered a church planting superstar. He has the fastest growing church in his city with no signs of slowing down anytime soon. Love Church is an overwhelming success. Or is it?

Remember the strategy-driving question that led to the launch of his successful church? "How can a church attract the people of this city and meet their needs in a practical way?" This is a great question, but Pastor Bill's answer has missed the mark.

Love Church has attracted people because the charismatic preacher has turned the pulpit into a self-help soapbox. Sermon series are based on the latest plot lines from network TV and popular movies. The main point of every talk is how to become the best _____ you can be (businessman/woman, friend, husband, wife, parent …). For those who are poor and needy, Pastor Bill offers the hope that bigger faith will lead to a bigger bank account. To the wealthy and satisfied, Pastor Bill offers guilt-free accrual of stuff because, after all, material wealth is a sign of an acceptable faith.

The church has grown because it has catered to people in every way, shape, and form. Sin, a term creatively avoided by anyone on Pastor Bill's stage, is always corporate and never personal. The Bible is recast as a book about love—only instead of God's word of truth and love, every culturally offensive part of the Bible has been removed in order to be culturally acceptable to people.[15] Pastor Bill's goal has been achieved. People actually like church again. What's wrong with that?

---

15. The New Testament word to describe such syncretists is *Sadducee*. A sect of Judaism that differed wildly from the Pharisees, the Sadducees believed that decisions of right and wrong were not based on God's moral standard, but were choices ultimately left for each individual (see Flavius Josephus, *Jewish War* 2.164–66; *Jewish Antiquities* 13.297–98). This view is not surprising when you consider that the Sadducees believed only in the first five books of the Old Testament and didn't believe in eternal judgment, hell, and resurrection (see Mark 12:18–27).

Well, just about everything. The good news you hear at Love Church has really little to do with the good news about Jesus — his life, death, and resurrection.

Ditch 2: Sectarianism

A second ditch that the church can fall into is called *sectarianism*. Sectarianism occurs when the authority of the church is elevated above the authority of Scripture, as we see in Figure 4.2.

Sectarianism
FIGURE 4.2

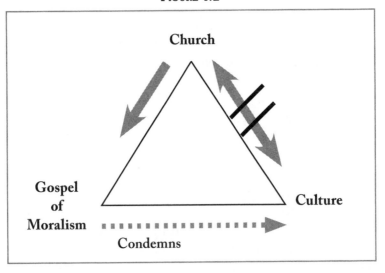

Figure 4.2 shows us the priorities of the sectarian church. As indicated by the church holding the top position on the triangle, the sectarian church promotes the belief that the culture is an enemy that falls outside the scope of God's redemptive work, and it espouses the false gospel of moralism. Not only does the sectarian church misrepresent the true gospel by preaching a gospel of condemnation, it establishes an inherently antagonistic relationship between the church and culture.

Whereas syncretism tends to be the sin of the "liberal church," sectarianism is commonly the sin of the "conservative church." This is because conservative leaning churches tend to redefine sin so it is almost exclusively about external behaviors. Instead of focusing on the internal problem — the heart's worship of anything other than God — sectarians rearticulate the gospel as rules to follow rather than grace to receive. Consider yet another "story" that is all too real in many churches today.

Offended by everything from "those TV shows today" to tattoos and piercings of wayward young people, First Self-Righteous Church[16] prides itself on not being worldly. Avoiding sin is the primary goal of the church, and so members are encouraged to spend as much time as possible attending sin-free church functions, of which there is no shortage.

The preaching of the First Self-Righteous Church is heavy on the topic of sin, which is usually classified as the things that other people do. Grace is mentioned only to say, "by God's grace" we're not like "those people." Relationships with non-Christians are avoided because it is believed that if a Christian befriends a non-Christian, they will somehow "catch" their sins, sort of like you would catch the swine flu.

In fact, it is the "us" (the church) vs. "them" (the world) dichotomy that most clearly defines the sectarian church. The result is that the church pushes people who desperately need spiritual healing away from the only source that can help them — the gospel. Sectarians tend to hide out in Bible studies and immerse themselves in the Christian subculture in order to "grow in their faith" while avoiding the big, bad world on the outside. Sectarians are modern-day Pharisees who fail to emulate Jesus, who constantly involved himself with messy, sinful people to the point of being labeled their "friend" (Matt. 11:19; Luke 7:34).

Contextualization in the Hands of Gospel-Saturated Churches

Figure 4.3 shows us a healthy model of contextualization. In this diagram, the gospel is on top of the triangle, which means

---

16. Full credit to legendary songwriter and satirist Ray Stevens for the perfect sectarian church name!

that both the culture and the church submit to the authority of the gospel. A church *for* the city, most simply, is a church that practices healthy contextualization. It's a church that soaks in the Scriptures and is saturated with the gospel. The arrows show the flow of movement that carries along a gospel-saturated church.

The gospel message penetrates down deep into the church, like a marinade that flavors and tenderizes a piece of meat. A gospel-saturated church then takes the gospel into its culture. Submitted to and saturated with the gospel, the church does not have to fear the culture or become the culture, but it can influence the culture, redeeming it and presenting it back to God as an act of worship. Because the church is securely rooted in the gospel, it is free to consider the information it receives from culture and adapt its methods of gospel proclamation to most effectively influence the culture.

Healthy Contextualization
Figure 4.3

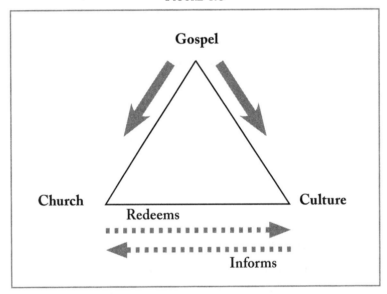

Both syncretists and sectarians fall into the trap of defining themselves by what they don't want to be instead of what they are in the gospel. Syncretists don't want to be offensive. Sectarians don't want to be "sellouts." The error of both is that they leave out the gospel, which says we are offensive to God because of sin,[17] but that Christ has come to redeem those are sinful.[18]

A church for the city will avoid both syncretism and sectarianism by clinging to the true gospel with its brutal truth and beautiful grace. And it will communicate the things people may not like hearing in a way that they can understand, so that when they hear the gospel of salvation it will be good news indeed.

As we close this chapter, let's look at a few of the practices of a church that authentically contextualizes the gospel for its city.

A gospel-saturated congregation proclaims that Jesus is Lord. The fundamental claim of Christianity is summed up by Paul in Romans 11:36: "From him and through him and to him are all things. To him be glory forever. Amen." Of course, the "him" is Jesus, and the radical nature of such a statement cannot be overemphasized. As Alan Hirsch says well, proclaiming that Jesus is comprehensively Lord, the one who reigns over every area of everything, touches "the epicenter of the biblical consciousness of God to which we must return if we are to renew the church in our day."[19]

A gospel-saturated congregation distills Christian life to a simple form: Jesus is Lord over every area of individual and corporate life. In other words, there is no safe haven from the scandalous invasion of Christ on any and every other claim to a Christian's loyalty. Not only does the radical claim of Jesus' lordship shape the theology, life, and practice of the church, but its simplicity makes it easy to pass on.

A gospel-saturated congregation knows itself, and, therefore, it knows how to enter into culture without losing its Christian distinctiveness. By telling, retelling, and rehearsing the true story of human longing

---

17. Romans 3:23, "For all have sinned and fall short of the glory of God."

18. Mark 2:17, "[Jesus] said to them, 'Those who are well have no need of a physician, but those who are sick. I came not to call the righteous, but sinners.'"

19. Alan Hirsch and Darryn Altclass, *The Forgotten Ways Handbook* (Grand Rapids: Brazos, 2009), 37.

and fulfillment found only in the gospel, followers of Jesus know their true identity in Christ and are able to interpret the prevailing cultural ethic, ideas, philosophies, art, and stories in light of the gospel. Therefore, modern-day missionaries maintain appropriate moral boundaries within culture because they view prevailing cultural values with healthy skepticism. Good missionaries see how cultural values serve merely to point people toward the *ultimate* fulfillment and purpose that is only found in Christ.

A gospel-saturated congregation knows its neighborhood. It knows how the people they are trying to reach define "good news." They ask questions like:

- What are the dominant values of this neighborhood and how does the gospel redeem or reject these values?
- What are the "third places" in my neighborhood where people gather for community and conversation?
- What are the unique political, zoning, educational, and commercial concerns of the people in my neighborhood?

A gospel-saturated church is a church that exists not for itself but for its city, neighborhood, and block. In fact, the whole point of contextualization is to determine how the folks in a given context might most naturally understand and receive the gospel. Contextualization is an inherently "other-centered" exercise because it forces a missionary to consider those outside the church in order to provide a welcoming environment for them inside the church. A church for its city must continuously assess whether it is accounting for the uniqueness and eccentricities of its neighborhoods as it seeks to minister to it. Questions to ask continually are:

- What does good news look/sound like in my neighborhood?
- How does the gospel address the longings for good news expressed by the people in my neighborhood and/or city?
- Am I portraying the gospel as the reportage of vibrant news of something that actually happened in history and has immediate and future impact, or as a dusty, old religion

that may or may not change the way one sees the present and future?

A church for its city contextualizes the gospel to those they want to reach, even if the target group is not yet represented within the congregation. It's what I call the "Field of Dreams Principle": "If you preach it, they will come." In other words, if you preach as if there are non-Christians in your seats, soon there will be. If you preach as if there are artists or jocks or young parents or movie buffs in your church, there soon will be. This is the beauty of preaching the pure gospel. It is always for the benefit of believers and nonbelievers. If Christians are to grow, they need to hear and apply the gospel. If those far from God are to be brought near, they need to hear and apply the gospel. Questions to ask are:

- Who lives in our area but is not represented in our church? Senior citizens, young families, singles, the urban poor and needy, the urban wealthy and self-satisfied?
- Who in our current congregation is positioned to best reach the group or groups of people God is calling us to reach?

Churches must return, again and again, to the heart of the gospel for renewal and for empowerment in order to proclaim it confidently to the culture. A gospel-saturated church seeking the good of its city will continually return to these five practices. This is a continuous process, not simply a one-time event. A church that fails to reflect on these key questions noted above will eventually move away from the gospel and begin following a cultural agenda or the personal agenda of its leaders. Either way, they will have lost the heart of God's agenda—gospel truth delivered to the culture through the church in a way that leads to transformation and renewal.

CHAPTER 5

Community (Darrin)

Community in the Garden

The cinematic spectacular *Jerry Maguire* was one of the top five grossing movies of 1996. Along with its ability to draw women with the romantic story line and men with the "insider's" look at the business of professional sports, *Jerry Maguire* also gave us a remarkable look at our culture's fascination with and general misunderstanding of relationships. In one of the film's most famous scenes, Jerry, played by Tom Cruise, and Dorothy Boyd, played by Renee Zellweger, are at the ultimate crossroads in their on-again-off-again romantic relationship. In a last-ditch effort to profess his deep feelings for Dorothy, Jerry begins one of the most memorable (and most highly idealized) exchanges in recent cinematic history.

> *Jerry:* I love you. You ... you complete me. And I just...
> *Dorothy:* Shut up. Just shut up. You had me at "hello."[1]

As we will soon see, Jerry was only half right.

It is my contention that the most effective way to know God more intimately is to be in deep relationships with other Christians who are also seeking to know God intimately. How can I make such a sweeping statement about knowing God and the value of Christian community? The answer begins by asking some additional questions.

What is your model for relationship? What is your ideal for authentic, meaningful community? Some of us had really good family systems where healthy relationships were effectively modeled. Some of us have friendships that have existed ever since both individuals had snotty noses and dirty diapers. Many of us have

---

1. *Jerry Maguire*, DVD, directed by Cameron Crowe (Gracie Films, 1996).

high school or college friends that we text with, tweet with and about, Facebook, talk to, and get together with.

Personally, I have experienced a legitimately intimate, beautiful relationship with my wife, Amie. We have been through struggles where without the support and encouragement we provided each another, despondency and dejection might have won the day. I can honestly say that our marriage bond has inspired and challenged me more than any human relationship I have ever had.

But as good and transformative as my marriage relationship has been, it is not my primary model for deep, abiding relationship.

So, again, I ask, What is your model for relationship?

Regardless of your relationship experiences, the true model for community is not found in the home we grew up in, no matter how nurturing and encouraging. Our model for community is not found in our lifelong friendship with the kid we grew up with, no matter how loyal they have been or how rich our relational history. Our relationship model cannot ultimately come from even the healthiest of marriages. And authentic relationship is certainly not modeled by "chick flick theology." In *Jerry Maguire*, we know that when Jerry tells Dorthy that she "completes" him, they are talking exclusively about romantic companionship. As much as this resonates within us, we know that true and lasting community is more than romance.

The perfect model that meets our longing for relationship is not found by looking horizontally, within the community of *humanity*. Instead, it is found by looking vertically—at the community of *divinity*. God, by nature, is community. God, by nature, is relational. And we know this is true because of the Trinity.

To talk about God as a Trinity means that God is three distinct persons and each person is fully God. The persons of the Trinity are distinct in the ways they relate to one another and to creation, but they are all one God. Within one undivided being there unfold interpersonal relationships such that there are three distinct persons. This three-person God has existed forever within the perfect community we call the Trinity, dwelling in perfect love, appropriate submission, and eternal glory.

Imagine with me back to the beginning of time as we know it. One day, for reasons we don't fully understand, this triune God decided to create. Everything that God created was good: mountains, moon, seas, and sun. God pronounced a benediction — literally a "good word" — over his creation, and everything was just as God desired it (Gen. 1:25). Then this triune God said, "Let us make man in our own image" (Gen. 1:26),[2] and Adam was made.

After creating Adam, though, we note something interesting as the Genesis account unfolds. Now, for the first time in created history, God says that something is *not* good: "Then the LORD God said, 'It is not good that the man should be alone'" (Gen. 2:18a). Was this because God had made an error in Adam's design? No! Adam was created to relate perfectly with God, to talk and walk with him in the garden. No, the problem was not with Adam's design. The problem was not even with Adam. The problem was that it was *just* Adam. It was "not good" for Adam to be *alone*.

It was an intentional part of the way that God chose to design Adam, to help him understand and recognize that he was not yet complete: "I will make him a helper fit for him" (Gen. 2:18b). The first thing God makes that is *not* good is a person living without an appropriate human relationship. Even though Adam had perfect fellowship with God, shockingly, this was not enough to qualify as "good."

We know that when God says it is not good for us to be alone, he is not talking about having times where we practice solitude and withdraw from human community for meditation and reflection. Jesus himself endorsed and practiced solitude (Matt. 4:1–11; Mark 1:12–13). The incompleteness of Adam was more than just being physically alone. Adam was not yet complete because by himself he could not fully reflect the God who had made him. It was not good for Adam to be alone, not because God failed to make him good, but because God made him so that Adam would

---

2. This is the literal translation of the Hebrew and is the first glimpse we see of the Trinity in the Bible.

reflect God's own image, and that reflection was not complete in Adam alone. Creation reflects God's order, his beauty, his diversity, and his glory. And God intended for Adam to reflect the relational, multifaceted nature of the triune God.

So God created Eve in such a way that they, together, could image God and reflect him to the creation. Eve was made to complement Adam, just as Adam was created to complement his future wife. In this way human beings reflect God—not a solitary being who lives in isolation, but a being who eternally exists in intimate, perfect fellowship.[3]

The Doctrine of the Trinity

I realize that the doctrine of the Trinity often creates problems for Christians when they try to explain it. If you don't know what I mean, then you haven't tried to explain the Trinity to an unbeliever or a new Christian. You'll likely get lots of questions! How can Jesus be God when he calls himself the Son of God? How can Jesus be God when he talked with God? Is the Holy Spirit really a ghost?

But offering inadequate analogies to explain the Trinity is probably not the best way to grasp the relational nature of a triune God. To really "get" the Trinity you have to see the beauty of the triune relationships. The best analogies that help us understand this are not those from the world of science or art, but those that come from the context of our own human relationships. There is a reason why God says that it's "not good" for human beings to lack deep companionship. Our creation in God's image suggests that we most fully reflect the triune God when we are in deep, abiding relationships. These relationships reverse the "not-goodness" of being alone.[4]

---

3. See Anthony A. Hoekema, *Created in God's Image* (Carlisle, UK: Paternoster, 1986), for an excellent treatment of this subject.

4. A theological term that helps us understand the relationships between the Trinity is "economic Trinity." This terms deals with how the three persons in the Godhead relate to each other and the world. Each has different roles within the

The "gods" of most other religions are not personal and relational. Instead, you will find an impersonal god who doesn't weep, express emotion, speak, or have a will to act or choose. This "god" is nothing like the God of the Bible. It's more akin to the Force from Star Wars, a vague sort of energy that moves without consciousness or clear intention. An impersonal god is, by definition, not someone (or something) you can have a real relationship with. He (it) lacks personhood.

In Islam, we find a God who *is* personal, but is not *tri*-personal as we find in the Trinity. The God of Islam is unipersonal, which means that he eternally relates only to himself—a single being. A unipersonal God is by nature nonrelational and self-reflective. This is, in fact, what Muslims teach and believe, that God has always existed in isolation—until he decided to create: planets, angels, and people. In Islam, God's relational nature is secondary, a result of his decision to create. But it is not an essential part of his eternal being.

In fact, apart from the trinitarian God of the Bible, all other world religions view relationship as something secondary to God's being: a peripheral, nonessential aspect of his nature. In every other religious belief system, God's relationship with human beings—if there is one—is something extra and optional, the icing on the cake. In these religious expressions, relationship does not seriously affect the very being and nature of God.

But this is not true with the God of the Bible. The Scriptures reveal to us a triune God who exists in coequal and coeternal relationships within himself. This means that God did not create because he was lonely and needed a friend. God did not create other beings because he was lacking anything relationally. As the eternal Father, Son, and Spirit, God has enjoyed perfect love, perfect communion, and perfect relationship forever!

When God said to the first man, "Adam, it is not good for you to be alone, so I am going to make a partner for you," God was teaching Adam something true and beautiful about God's own

---

Godhead and each has different roles in relationship to the world. Though some roles overlap at times, a basic way to understand this is to say, "The Father sent the Son, the Son sent the Spirit, the Spirit indwells and sanctifies the church."

nature—something Adam needed to know and experience for himself. And when Adam first met his helper, that moment inspired powerful emotions. The first poem in human history poured forth from Adam's lips as he sang out: "This at last is bone of my bone and flesh of my flesh" (Gen. 2:23). While it may not sound like Top Forty material to us today, this single line from Adam's song tells us everything we need to know about reflecting God in our relationship with others. Adam is saying to his created companion: "In Eve I have found myself. This beautiful woman is from me, and she complements me. I now know more of who God has made me to be because I have a companion." Only in relationship with others can we fully understand who God has made us to be.

C. S. Lewis beautifully articulates this point in a touching story in his book *The Four Loves*. He describes his closest circle of friends, a circle that included J. R. R. Tolkien and the great British novelist, poet, and theologian Charles Williams. Charles died suddenly in 1945, and his death had a profound effect on Lewis. Reflecting on the impact of Charles's life and his sudden passing, Lewis realized that he'd assumed that since Charles was now dead, as awful as that fact was, he could take some consolation in the fact that he'd now have *more* of his friend Ronald (Tolkien). With Charles no longer there, he and Ronald would be able to spend more time together, have more conversations together, and have more shared experiences.

But to his shock and dismay, Lewis realized that just the opposite came true. In losing Charles he found that he did not have more of Ronald, but less of him. In losing Charles he lost that part of Ronald that only Charles could bring out. Lewis writes, "No one human being can bring out all of another person, but it takes a whole circle of human beings (community) to extract the real you."[5] Lewis continues,

> In each of my friends there is something that only some other friend can fully bring out. By myself I am not large enough

---

5. C. S. Lewis, *The Four Loves* (New York: Harcourt Brace, 1991), 61.

to call the whole man into activity. I need other lights than my own to show all my friend's facets.... In this, friendship exhibits a glorious "nearness by resemblance" to Heaven itself, where the very multitude of the blessed (which no man can number) increases the fruition which each has of God.[6]

Lewis is highlighting a key point of this chapter—that we come to know God more intimately in healthy, intimate relationships with other Christians who are also seeking to know God. The multiple facets of who we are can only be uncovered in community, and despite what popular culture tells us, we were not meant to "find ourselves" on our own. As individuals, we can't mine the depths of our greatest hopes, our worst fears, and the deepest desires of our hearts. Living in community and close relationship with other people reveals our strengths—that which makes us helpful to others—as well as our weaknesses—those things that makes us hurtful, our sinful patterns of behavior.

Relationships grow and mature us. We find authentic community as we learn to experienced Christ *through* one another. Biblical community is experienced as we come to know others and are known by them, love and are loved, serve and are served, celebrate and are celebrated in return.[7]

Although the disobedience of Adam led to a fracture in human relationships, the story line of salvation reminds us that God has not abandoned his original intentions for us. The revelation of the Old and New Testaments shows us a consistent pattern of God's seeking us, saving us, and reconciling our broken relationships with him and with each other. God initiated a covenant with Abraham because he desired to be in community with him and his descendants, and he desired for Abraham and his descendants to uniquely experience what it is like to commune with the divine. The incarnation of God in the person of Jesus Christ is the fulfillment of this reconciling work, because in it God established

---

6. Ibid., 62.

7. I heard this definition of community in a talk given by Bill Hybels at the 1997 Leadership Summit.

an eternal covenant relationship with sinful human beings—not through another sinful man (like Abraham), but through the perfect, sinless God-man, Jesus. Divine community has now come down to dwell among us, and one day we will live in perfect community with God and each other forever.

Until that day, God offers us a foretaste of his divine community as we experience life with him through the work of the Spirit, who indwells each believer. As believers come together, reconciled to God and one another through the work of the triune God and empowered by the Spirit, we witness the human expression of the divine community—the church. In the church, God displays his relational nature to the world. And like a telescope, which uses both a primary lens and a magnifying lens to bring clarity to objects we could never be able to see on our own, the community of the church exists to magnify that which is primary: the glory of God in the person of Jesus Christ.

Community for the City

Community-based entertainment became vogue in the 1980s and 1990s through situational comedies like *Cheers*, *Friends*, and *Seinfeld*. These shows helped cement the very Western idea that people who are similar in life stage, economic bracket, and entertainment interests could authentically connect as individuals, and as a result be connected to something bigger than themselves. The characters in these sitcoms mimicked the world at large by expressing a desire to be recognized and identified by the similarities they shared with others—their friends. These shared desires and interests created what we call *affinity*.

Affinity is simply that sense of belonging that happens when people surround themselves with people who are like them, generally for the purpose of reminding all parties involved how great they are. We see this when people gather to celebrate their favorite sports team or to remember a common cultural heritage. Due to the organization of the urban environment, pure affinity relationships are less common because there are higher concentrations of diverse people living in close proximity to one another. In rural and suburban areas affinity-based relationships are more common because there is less diversity and more space for people to spread out. You can literally avoid people by owning a big piece of land or by shutting the garage door of your minikingdom. But that's much harder in the city. When you live in a city you are forced, often uncomfortably so, to rub shoulders with people who don't look like you, smell like you, or think like you—but they may live within spitting distance of your front door.

Likewise, because your primary spheres of life, work, play, and home are in the city, they are more likely to be proximate, making it much easier to integrate all of your life with your most significant relationships. In the city, it is likely that you will have the same people involved with you in every sphere of life: work, play, and home. This is often in contrast to life in a suburban or rural environment, where housing and commerce are purposely zoned apart from each other. In the suburbs, people may not have meaningful opportunities to interact with people of different races, socioeconomic statuses, or interests.

A church *for* a city must wrestle with the question: How do you best leverage the opportunities the city provides for authentic, gospel-centered community? It's a great question to ask wherever you live, even if you aren't living in a city right now. Wherever you are called, it is essential that you equip your people to understand the true values of biblical community and that you are looking for ways to promote relationships that don't rely on a "pseudo"-community born solely out of affinity.

Practical Examples of Community in the City

The primary metaphors that are used to describe the New Testament church are those of the household—the family of God—and the body (the "body of Christ"). Inherent in both of these metaphors is the theme of dependency. Family members depend on one another for food, income, instruction, entertainment, conversation, and a whole host of other things. Similarly, in order to function properly, the body depends on each of the parts of the body—the various limbs and organs—working together in unison. We know that our bodies need blood for survival. Yet the proper functioning of blood is itself dependent on the lungs to bring in the oxygen and the heart to pump it through the body.

As followers of Christ, we understand that ultimately, all that we have and need comes from Christ. We depend on Christ for everything, not the least of which is our salvation. But we also depend on Christ to be the *source* of authentic community.[8] As the head of the body, Christ is also the source of what we need to function as a healthy body. Christ both guides the church and provides it with the nutrition—the spiritual sustenance—it needs to survive and mature. A key ingredient in Christ's meal plan for his people is that we regularly feast on Christ-imitating community.

One of the primary responsibilities of a church that wants to exist *for* its city is helping people see that there are people hungry for real biblical community in their places of work, home, and play. By promoting and living out biblically rooted community where each of us work, live, and play, we draw people toward the gospel—the message they so desperately need.

Where You Work

A church for the city will equip people to see that their *workplace* is full of people who need the kind of community that only the gospel can offer.

The owner of OK Used Cars in St. Louis is a member of The Journey. Joe Kaminski loves Jesus, loves the church, and loves the unique adventure that is the used car business. He sees no reason why all those things can't blend together. Joe "gets it." The call of a missionary—taking the gospel into an environment where it is not yet flourishing—isn't lost on him. As a result, OK Used Cars is a place where you can both see and hear the gospel. If OK Used

---

8. Ephesians 5:23, "Christ is the head of the church, his body, and is himself its Savior" (see also 1 Cor. 12:27; Eph. 1:22–23; Col. 1:18).

Cars closed its doors today, a gospel light in St. Louis would be snuffed out.

Because of Joe's easy-going missionary style, he effortlessly breathes the gospel to people. Some say he talks about it too much, but to some — a growing number of people — the gospel he speaks about has become less about "just the way Joe is" and more about Jesus. It is a message that has the power to change lives.

Some of Joe's employees started getting together to read the Bible because they kept hearing Joe talk about it. They figured they'd rather look at it for themselves than go to church, which most guys working at the car lot had rejected since their youth. These times of reading the Bible together eventually grew into a full-blown Bible study that is now attended not just by the employees of OK Used Cars, but by friends and several Journey regulars who want to be a part of something outside the norm: a simple, grassroots gathering of believers and people looking for answers in the Bible.

Ross Jordan is the facilities director at the Journey and is also one of the group's leaders. He loves the study because it is aimed at guys, just like the guy he used to be. "These are neighborhood guys that grew up in the inner city. Some of them have a pretty jaded past, but they've gotten to a point in their life where they kind of want to do away with all of that. I understand those dudes because I *was* that dude."

One story from Ross captures how many of the men are beginning to experience a new sense of freedom in studying and talking about the gospel:

> The kind of guys we're trying to reach are like Hollywood, Richie, and Johnny. I met Johnny through the party scene when I was sixteen or seventeen. I happened to be at the car lot one day to get my wife's car fixed. While I'm standing there talking to Joe, out of the corner of my eye I see this guy walking, and he was looking real hard at me, and it's Johnny standing there.

We looked at each other, and I was thinking I know that guy, but he looks like he's put on a few pounds.

We talked for a few minutes, and he told me he had some kids now and he suggested we ought to get together. I kind of agreed, but I was thinking, "Man, I don't know where this guy's at with his life. He might be setting me up to rob my house or something."

Johnny and I talked for a bit and he told me that Joe, the owner of the lot, had been talking to him and had led him to Christ. From that point on I was 100 percent involved in the Bible study. I was all in. I had written all those guys from my old neighborhood off. I was like Jonah. I didn't want anything to do with bringing the gospel into that situation.

Since all that, Johnny told me he feels more comfortable in the group because he's more comfortable with his Bible. Now he's not so worried about his life and his past but is wanting to help other guys like him get more out of God's Word.

And Johnny is still connected to a lot of guys from the old neighborhood, so we're now trying to figure out how to get back in touch with some of these guys and ultimately share the gospel with them. I don't know how all that is going to play out yet, but I didn't know that any of this stuff was going to happen with me or Johnny either.

The thing I love about what's happening through the car lot is it's not just about being cordial with somebody, asking them how they're doing when you don't actually care how they're doing. I feel compelled to get out there and try to reach people that a lot of other people are avoiding. Apart from the fact that I love Jesus, I'm not really any different from the guys we're trying to reach, at least in terms of my past. But that love for Jesus changes me, so I don't have to come at these dudes spitting out Bible verses.

After I get to know them and we've hung out for a while and built a relationship and there's trust there and they know that I genuinely care about them, they see Christ reflected through me. Then I've given them a reason to hear the gospel, and I am confident that I can communicate it to them in a way not too many people can.

At the time of this printing, the Bible study has been going strong for nearly two years. The requirements are simple: show up, and if you've got a Bible, bring it. If you don't, you'll get one at the group, and you open it up. That's it.

The Bible study at OK Used Cars reminds us that the workplace is not off-limits to a true missionary. It is simply one more place to share the gospel with people who need to hear it. The quotable Ross Jordan sums up what's happening at OK Used Cars.

> We are constantly trying to remind the guys in the group that it's not about your good deeds. Jesus is not only your conduit, your link to God, but he was perfect because you can't be. He came and died because he knows you're a sinner. Your job is to trust him and accept the fact that he loves you and wants to change you. That's where a lot of these guys' ears perk up, and they're like, "Is it really that simple?" I tell them it's simple and it's challenging. But it's a good challenge, the best kind of challenge. It's what life is really all about.

Where You Live

A church for the city will also equip people to see that their neighborhood (apartment complex, school dorm, or condo) is full of people longing for the kind of community that only the gospel can offer.

In *The Forgotten Ways Handbook*, Alan Hirsch describes the incarnation of Jesus this way: "He took human form and moved into the neighborhood."[9] A church for the city will release everyday missionaries loose into their neighborhoods so that they can bring to their neighbors a taste of gospel-centered community.

At The Journey we have tried a variety of different approaches to create these small, gospel-driven communities in our

---

9. Alan Hirsch and Darryn Altclass, *The Forgotten Ways Handbook* (Grand Rapids: Brazos, 2009), 88.

neighborhoods. The latest iteration (and so far the most effective) is what we call "missional communities." Our missional communities are the primary way we are helping people live out their call to advance the gospel in their neighborhoods. Here's a quick sketch of how these groups work in our church and city.

Our missional communities are created with a simple goal: helping people get over their instincts to stick together and form a "holy huddle" and empower them to boldly set out on a missionary journey to love and serve their own neighborhood. Our missional communities do have occasions where they turn inwardly, but only for a time. Typically, they are made up of members who live near each other geographically, and as a group they gather to pray for their neighbors, share wins and setbacks in their relationships with their non-Christian neighbors, and receive collective training from each other about how to continue seeding the gospel in the soil of their own "backyard." The inward-focused times of meeting together serve the essentially outward focus of the group. At the heart, these are groups with a mission to reach their neighbors with the gospel.

It all sounds simple, and in many ways it is, and intentionally so. Our missional communities purposefully hold to a simple structure in order to keep people focused on their neighbors rather than the church. The common temptation in the American church is to neglect the world in order to protect the church. At The Journey we also experience this temptation, and so we live with a keen awareness that yielding to this temptation results in a bunch of Christians who, instead of being "bought-in" — loving and serving their neighbors — are mostly "checked-out" from their neighborhoods, closing themselves up in a sanctuary several hours a week rather than opening their home to share dinner with unbelievers who live right next door.

Here are a few of the things we have learned to *do* in our missional communities and some things we have learned to *avoid* as we seek to train and empower a church full of neighborhood missionaries eager to share and live out the gospel right where they live.

- *Don't* underestimate the power of prayer.
- *Do* pray often for your neighborhood.

Among other benefits, prayer reminds you that the monumental task of reaching your neighborhood with the gospel is an act of the Spirit, not something that is ultimately dependent on your own human effort. Our missional communities pray together in a variety of different ways and in various settings. One missional community has a group that jogs together at 6:00 a.m. every Wednesday morning. Because they are too busy huffing and puffing to talk, they find that it's the perfect time to pray together for their neighborhood. This is also a good practice because it literally brings the neighborhood into view for them. Members of this group have told me that the Spirit sometimes leads them to pray for a specific household over several weeks.

- *Don't* go it alone.
- *Do* promote vital relationships between the Christ followers in your community.

Of the many countercultural requirements of the gospel, few are as offensive to people today as the concept of *dependency*. The heroes of our American culture are men and women who are able to go it alone and "pull themselves up by their own boot straps," forging their own path ahead. This "Lone Ranger" ethic clashes with the ethic of Christian discipleship, a life submitted to and dependent on Jesus Christ and the daily filling of God's Spirit.

Scripture teaches us that the Christian community can be likened to a house made of stone (1 Peter 2:5–6). Jesus is the cornerstone that sets the level and guides the fit of all the other stones, while individual Christians are the "living stones" fitted together to make a durable "spiritual house." The stones of this building are so connected, so *dependent* on one another, that if one stone were removed, it would affect the other stones that are connected to it. They would simply tumble to the ground, dependent on the support that had been removed. John Stott's good friend John Wyatt says it this way, "God's design for our life is that we should be dependent."[10] If we wish to be a blessing to our neighborhoods, we first must learn to bless each other and rely on one another.

Our missional communities must somehow try to factor the following practical values into the community culture they are attempting to establish.

Members create enough margin in their lives that they could gather with other members of the group at a moment's notice. Hirsch puts it well. "Clever mission groups anticipate spontaneity and realize it is crucial to be adaptable and responsive."[11]

Members see their homes *not* as places of retreat but as ministry centers. Group members know they have a home base for prayer, encouragement, and hospitality at any of the other member's homes.

Members see their interactions with each other as an opportunity to bless unbelievers. Individual evangelism is an integral part of Christian discipleship, but our communities strive to introduce (or reintroduce) people to Christ through a real-life example of healthy Christian community.

- *Don't* play it safe.
- *Do* take risks.

Here is the reality for a true disciple of Jesus. Following him will *always* take you into relationships that make you uncomfortable. In other words, if you are not currently in some kind of relationship with a drunk, a prostitute, a beggar, an outcast, or a modern social equivalent to one of these people, you are not wholeheartedly following Jesus.

The problem with many small group ministries is that they play it safe and fail to account for the reality that the missional life is a life of risk. While this seems scary — and often is — the truth is that there can be no serious missional impact without a willing-

---

10. John Stott, *The Radical Disciple: Some Neglected Aspects of Our Calling* (Downers Grove, IL: InterVarsity Press, 2010), 110.

11. Hirsch and Altclass, *The Forgotten Ways Handbook*, 96.

ness to move out of the cozy confines of the sanctuary and into the unknown relationships that God calls us to pursue.

This is what Peter assumed in 1 Peter 2:11–12 when he reminded Christians that they are "sojourners and exiles" in this world. Peter is not implying that Christians should huddle together and keep the "big bad world" at bay. Instead, he is saying that as you enter into relationships that are uncomfortable for you keep in mind the big picture. Ultimately, you can be comforted by the reality that you have been reborn by the Spirit, you are made for a world that is yet to come, and one day Christ will be the undisputed King of the universe. With this eternal comfort and perspective, you are free to enter into uncomfortable relationships with people with whom you may share nothing in common.

What's more, Peter says, you can actually have a positive influence in your neighborhood by keeping your "conduct among the Gentiles honorable." When you are willing to live as a person with an eternal hope, boldly entering into relationships and establishing a gospel presence in the lives of those who witness your behavior every day, you are taking risks similar to those first disciples who followed Christ's example.

- *Don't* assimilate or separate from culture.
- *Do* live distinct but be engaged, seeking the flourishing of your city.

During the Babylonian exile in the sixth century BC, God's people were strangers in a strange land. God used the prophet Jeremiah to communicate that he valued cultures and cities. Jeremiah didn't order God's people to withdraw from the enemy land they now called home. Jeremiah didn't tell people to hate their pagan neighbors. In what was certainly stunning news to the captives, God spoke to Jeremiah and instructed his people to *love* the city.

Build houses and live in them; plant gardens and eat their produce. Take wives and have sons and daughters; take wives for your sons, and give your daughters in marriage, that they may bear sons and daughters; multiply there, and do not decrease.

But seek the welfare of the city where I have sent you into exile, and pray to the LORD on its behalf, for in its welfare you will find your welfare. (Jer. 29:5–7 [emphasis added])

God's heart is for the cities and the cultures of people in those cities. Moreover, he has charged his followers, his church, to cultivate the well-being of the city—not just to bless the city, but for the very health of the church. Being cultivators of culture for the benefit of our cities is, God says, a pathway to our own welfare. Through prayer, through active presence and life-sharing, we can bless our cities for the glory of God, the benefit of society, and the benefit of the church.

Where You Play

When you think about the places where history-shaping, culture-transforming events begin, your mind probably goes immediately to images of battlefields, executive boardrooms, or podiums overlooking hundreds of thousands of people eager to receive an important message from a charismatic speaker. And these backdrops have definitely earned their place in history. But over the centuries, one setting consistently emerges as a breeding ground for the monumental pivot points of history: the pubs.

The British called them "public houses," a term that has since been shortened to "pub." Bar, tavern, ale house, lounge, saloon, watering-hole, night club ... all of these terms are used to describe a drinking establishment, a place that is licensed to serve alcoholic beverages. But the original public houses of Western Europe were more than just places to party and "hook-up"; they were the places where people gathered to converse, celebrate, mourn, and even plan world-changing revolutions.[12] The Irish called their public houses "shared living rooms."

---

12. David McCullough, *John Adams* (New York: Simon & Schuster, 2001). In this outstanding biography of the second president of the United States, McCullough shows plenty of evidence for the use of pubs and taverns as planning centers for the declaration of war against the British, the plans for independence, and development of war strategies.

Over the centuries, the church has tried to move the location of the "shared living room" from the pub to the sanctuary. In general, though, non-Christians who are regulars at the bars have not been convinced that they can trade up by exchanging their barstool for a church pew. This is what led several of us at The Journey to begin a ministry rooted in cultural engagement. We call it "Midrash."[13] Midrash's defining event is something known as "Theology at the Bottleworks," a monthly discussion about how the gospel sheds light on relevant cultural issues. Our goal is to engage non-Christians on issues that are relevant to them without forcing Christianity down people's throats.

As the name suggests, Theology at the Bottleworks (or TATB) is hosted at the Schlafly Bottleworks, a local microbrewery and restaurant. TATB allowed us the opportunity to have intelligent conversations with those who don't yet believe in Christ's power to save sinners. Since people were already gathering at the pub, the environment was not threatening to them. We were able to encourage the bar patrons to turn their barstools around and, instead of spending an evening alone drinking, join a stimulating conversation, a conversation that could serve as an introduction to the gospel.

Assuming that you are interested in doing some type of cultural engagement (which you should be), let me offer some questions you will want to consider as you seek to take the gospel into your city's areas of play and entertainment.

- Where are the people of your city or neighborhood already coming together for play?
- What conversations are people having as they gather? Are they discussing politics, movies, sports, music, etc.?
- Are you equipped to easily identify how the gospel affects the conversations people are having? If not, are you seeking training in this area?

---

13. The Hebrew word *midrash*, in its verbal root, literally means "to study" or "to investigate," and as a noun it means "commentary."

- Are you willing to be patient with those whose views on religion and morality differ from yours? Are you able to be gracious with non-Christians even if they are hostile to your most valued beliefs?

Community is not easy because relationships are complicated. And Christian community is not easy because Christians are complicated, saved but still sinful. That's why true, biblical community is so rare. And even rarer is a Christian community that sets its focus on the welfare of its city and not just the welfare of its church. Churches that exist for their cities will pray for strength and perseverance to do the hard work as they seek to become agents of grace. Not only do we need God's help in this endeavor, but we can't do it without him. We've been assured, however, that the God who is in himself perfect community can work in and through us to be a community that reflects God's heart for the people in our cities.

CHAPTER 6

Serving the City (Darrin)

A church for the city serves its city.
This statement may sound obvious, but serving your city takes more thought and hard work than you initially plan. The vision stage of serving your city is generally high on virtue and ideals and low on details and strategy. A church for the city is a church that is willing to roll up its sleeves and bring the vision down from the soaring 30,000-foot heights to ground level implementation.

The Journey's approach to serving our city began with a vision to address the brokenness we had encountered. The first practical step we made toward this worthy goal was to discern the needs of the people we wanted to serve in St. Louis. We found there were various needs we could invest our time and energy into, but as we prayed and considered them, we sensed God's leading in three particular areas of need in our city. God was calling us to provide:

- community development aimed at repairing the many *broken neighborhoods* in St. Louis.
- a ministry aimed at repairing the *broken relationship* between the church and St. Louis's many talented artists.
- Christian counseling to help repair the many *broken people* in our city.

Born out of this prayerful assessment of needs we developed three ministries: Mission: St. Louis, The Luminary Center for the Arts, and Karis House.

Mission: St. Louis[1]

Before Josh Wilson was a Journey pastor, he was a Journey intern with a heart to do mercy ministry with the urban poor in St. Louis. Great goal, difficult task.

Prior to starting his internship at The Journey, Josh saw first-hand the effects of poverty in St. Louis as he worked at a kids' sports camp in the urban core. His experiences at the sports camp led him to start a mercy ministry in July of 2006 at The Journey. After a three-month flurry of well-intended but unfocused activity, Josh realized that his team was attempting to do a lot of really good things, but they were failing miserably at all of them.

"We had built no relationships, shared no struggles, and carried no burdens with anyone we had served," Pastor Josh said. "We thought we knew what the poor needed without really listening to what they were saying." The turning point for Josh and the ministry came as they were working on yet another project—a school supply drive for the city schools. Among them was Adams Elementary in the Forest Park Southeast neighborhood, located a half mile from The Journey's Tower Grove campus in south St. Louis.

After the moderately successful school supply drive, Adams Elementary Principal Jeanetta Stegall met with Pastor Josh. Since Stegall was a leader in the Forest Park Southeast community, Pastor Josh asked her to suggest some other ways his team could help.

"If you could have anything you wanted, what would it be?" Josh asked.

The reply came immediately. Stegall shared her dream of a school where children had the family support they needed at home to help them succeed academically at school. She dreamed of having male role models in the neighborhood who could teach the boys how to be men. She dreamed of a school where families weren't forced to move because of the rising rent and gentrification. Ultimately, she wanted Adams Elementary to be a place where every child had a decent shot at reaching his or her full potential.

---

1. For more detailed information on these and other Mission: St. Louis ministries, please visit www.missionstl.org

As he listened to Principal Stegall, Josh began to realize that there was more to this relationship than he had first realized. He learned that Adams Elementary was essentially the hub of the Forest Park Southeast neighborhood. So his newly formed ministry, Mission: St. Louis, decided to put all its eggs in one basket, pouring their financial and human resources into serving Adams Elementary and the Forest Park Southeast neighborhood in the hope of transforming that one neighborhood, and from there transforming another, and another, and so on until real change was visible throughout St. Louis.

Today, Mission: St. Louis has grown beyond the scope of The Journey church and is now a 501(c)3 nonprofit that partners with churches all over the city promoting empowerment, education, and community development.

The most significant empowerment event for Mission: St. Louis is an "Affordable Christmas." In previous years, The Journey had participated in holiday programs that were entirely charity based. Volunteers bought gifts and delivered them to the families. But Pastor Josh noticed that something wasn't quite right as he was making a delivery run to a family. "I noticed that the kids, moms, and grandmas were ecstatic—smiling, laughing, crying, the whole nine yards. But the dads, if they were even there, did their best to sneak out the back door," he says. While charity was helpful in providing a decent Christmas for lots of kids, it was terrible at building up and empowering the family—and the men and fathers in particular.

Inspired by a program developed by Bob Lupton,[2] Josh began working with the Department of Family Services to identify low-income households in Forest Park Southeast and surrounding neighborhoods. With thousands of gifts donated by Journey members, Affordable Christmas focuses on empowerment rather than charity. It provides low-income parents an opportunity to shop and purchase gifts for their children at a low cost. Christmas is transformed for these families from a holiday filled with dread,

---

2. Robert D. Lupton, *Compassion, Justice and the Christian Life: Rethinking Ministry to the Poor* (Ventura, CA: Regal, 2007); previously published by CCDA Institute (2000) as *And You Call Yourself a Christian*.

worry, and disappointment to one of hope, joy, and pride. And all the money collected from toy sales goes right back into the FPSE neighborhood. In 2008 and 2009, the third and fourth annual Affordable Christmas events served more than 150 families and 600 children, with help from over 1,200 volunteers.

In addition to the Christmas event, a community Bible study takes place in the homes of Forest Park Southeast families and is led by indigenous community leaders, many of them coached by Mission: St. Louis and Journey volunteers. What started as a once-a-week meeting for a handful of Mission: St. Louis volunteers has since grown to a number of Bible studies in several homes on multiple nights of the week. Combined attendance has grown to more than a hundred participants.

To serve the community in the area of education, Mission: St. Louis developed the Morning Reading Program, a program designed by a graduate-level reading specialist and a Journey member, Brandy Greiner, in consultation with several literacy coaches in the St. Louis public schools. Volunteers spend twenty-five to thirty minutes reading with the children before the school day officially starts, and once a month they give each student a book to take home.

Finally, to help in developing the community, as of the time of this writing plans are underway to establish a donut and coffee shop in Forest Park Southeast that will provide jobs and a safe haven for authentic community-oriented relationships to grow and develop. Mission: St. Louis is also exploring opportunities to provide microfinancing that could help establish local businesses and create job opportunities for the poor and near-poor in St. Louis. Their ultimate goal is to empower local neighborhoods to be economically healthy, sustainable communities.

The Luminary Center for the Arts[3]

Most Christians don't often associate the church with great art. There may be an occasional singer who is talented, and you will

3. For more information about the Luminary Center for the Arts, please visit their website: theluminaryarts.com/.

certainly find musicians who can help lead worship; but often artists who work in other forms of media are ignored or marginalized by the church. Unless their art can be explicitly used in a worship service or as a sermon illustration, the gifts and talents of artists are typically not used in most churches.

But this was not always the case. The history of the church reminds us that the church was once the *primary* patron of artists. Some of the greatest works of art in human history were commissioned by the church, and some of the world's greatest artists were supported by the generosity of the Christian church. Churches that ignore or fail to utilize the gifts of artists are out of step with how the church has valued art for most of its history.

One Journey member saw this disconnect between the church and the artists in the St. Louis metro area, and he made it his life goal to do something about it. Former Journey intern and staff member James McAnally is familiar with both sides of the fence. A pastor's kid from Mississippi studying literature at Washington University in St. Louis, James was also an artist, relationally connected to other artists in St. Louis. And when I say artist, I'm not just talking about people who dabble here and there, but real, honest-to-goodness starving artists.

"I was an artist and a Christian, but could never connect these two groups because of the resistance and misunderstanding coming from the church side," says James. "Churches tend to use artists only for the decorating of the foyer. Artists tend to be activists and cultural catalysts, which makes most church leadership teams uncomfortable."

Instead of pounding his artistic fist on the table and demanding that The Journey elders commission sculptures for every corner of the sanctuary, James sought to repair the relationship between artists and churches by appealing to one of the core missions of the church: serving others.

"The formative idea behind The Luminary Center for the Arts was to give resources to artists, no questions asked—to think in terms of what artists need and then to do everything we could to meet those needs," James says. "I became passionate about that because I was in the community of artists in St. Louis, which is kind of an underground thing. I knew that artists needed affordable, even free studio space. They needed a place to show their art."

James pitched his idea for The Luminary to the elders, never expecting that anything would actually come of it. Much to his surprise, the elders not only went for it, offering verbal encouragement, but they also decided to throw some serious money at the idea. "My initial reaction was, 'Wow! Awesome!' Then I thought, 'What in the world have I gotten myself into? How are we going to make this work?'"

James and his newly established team set out to partner with as many different artist groups as possible, for the sole purpose of establishing relationships with artists all over the city. "You have to support other people's visions before you can expect them to support yours," advises James. "A good gauge of success for us is this: 'How many people in the art community trust us? Are they seeking to partner with us because we are a blessing to them? Do artists respect us?'"

James is now the executive director and founder of The Luminary Center for the Arts, which also has its own 501(c)3 status. Along with developing partnerships all over the city, The Luminary now offers St. Louis artists affordable studio and gallery space. Sensing that this was one of the greatest needs in the artistic community, The Journey and The Luminary partnered to convert a 9,000 square-foot former Catholic convent into gallery, studio, and event space on The Journey's Tower Grove campus. Along with art shows, The Luminary's Elevator Music Series hosts concerts by local and national acts, drawing scores of folks who would never think of attending a church. The space has received numerous accolades, including "Best New Multimedia Gallery" by the *Riverfront Times* and "Best Multipurpose Venue" by *St. Louis Magazine*.

But providing artists with space to work and showcase their art was just one goal of the ministry. The Luminary is best known for encouraging the formation of community and providing a creative environment for relationships to form through their funded artist residencies, which bring together some of the best emerging artists working in St. Louis and, increasingly, from around the world.

All of the attention the artists get and the awards are nice, but according to James, it's all just the icing on the cake. "Consistently, artists who have studios and even performers who are here for a one night opening or concert say to us that they never expected a church to do something like this. We've had resident artists who've attended church and heard the gospel for the first time in their lives. Some have finished their residencies and stated that they were 'blessed' by us. The word 'bless' was not even in their vocabulary before they met us.

"Artists observe the way we work with them and treat them, and they tell us there is something different about The Journey and The Luminary. When they ask what it is, I tell them it's like the first hospitals, when Christians were driven to help the sick and so they did it and others joined in. We're similar. Because in Christ we have been served in ways we never dreamed of, we are driven to serve artists, and others are seeing the need and benefit and finding ways to be a part of what God is doing through us."

Karis House[4]

Former Journey staff member Joel Greiner received his Masters of Arts in Counseling from Covenant Seminary in St. Louis. As a Licensed Professional Counselor (LPD), Joel took a job doing in-home crisis management with families who were in jeopardy of having children removed from their home because of alleged abuse.

"This was my first real introduction to the brokenness of the city and the families that live here," describes Greiner. "I saw what I was doing as a noble task, but after a while it became clear that my work was just a Band-Aid on a gaping wound. The root problems were never getting addressed. As a Christian, I knew that the real answer to all these problem relationships and scenarios was

---

4. For more information about Karis House, please visit the website, www.karishouse.org.

the gospel, but because I was working for a nonreligious organization, I wasn't allowed to bring my faith into my work."

His discontent with his work was surpassed only by the growing discontent he felt about the role the churches of St. Louis were playing in the lives of engaged couples, broken families, abused spouses and children, and addicts of all sorts.

"In 2005 I started coming to The Journey, which was definitely pro-Christian counseling. But because the church had no one to lead that effort, people were constantly being referred to outside counseling centers. I made myself known to some of the leaders and laid my cards on the table. I wanted to see what it would look like to begin providing affordable Christian counseling in the city, which was desperately needed but not adequately available."

With a green light from The Journey leaders and handling the counseling load himself, Joel quickly became overwhelmed with the number of clients and the depths of their needs. He responded by training a small army of lay counselors — some with degrees in counseling, most without. The lay counselors provided help for those who seemed to just want someone to talk to and pray with them.

The need soon emerged for even better trained counselors, so Joel partnered with Covenant Seminary to provide accredited field experience for students through The Journey's counseling ministry. When the influx of clients increased and as revenue allowed, Joel hired additional licensed counselors.

As the counseling army grew, the need for space to do the actual counseling became a major issue. As Joel said, "We began using Journey staff offices and about any semiprivate space we could find for sessions. Eventually, we knew that our twenty or so counselors needed more than five offices to give this thing a proper go."

Thus Karis House was born. The Journey purchased a dilapidated house adjacent to The Luminary Center for the Arts, and combined with fund-raising efforts and revenue from counseling sessions, the house was converted into a full-blown counseling center.

Joel is now the executive director, and Karis House is also a 501(c)3 that serves south St. Louis city by providing affordable, gospel-centered counseling and helping people restore relationships with God, family and friends, and themselves. The payment structure is based on a client's income. Most clients are paying between $10 and $20 for professional counseling, and counselors in training meet with people at no charge.

"Nobody can walk away from here because of money. That is never an issue. We trust that God will find a way for us to serve everyone who legitimately seeks help, and he has proven himself 100 percent trustworthy."

God has also proven himself trustworthy when it comes to transforming people's lives through the work being done at Karis House. Joel shares one example:

"We had a non-Christian guy come in with major anxiety issues. He had an intense phobia of crowded spaces. He couldn't get on an elevator with other people without having severe panic attacks. He was barely able to maintain his job. Then, on top of all that, he got a girl pregnant. He told me that when he saw his baby being born, he realized that there had to be some kind of God.

"He started coming to The Journey and began working through some of his issues in counseling. He became a Christian in one of our group counseling sessions. The best part of the story is that he got baptized in the summer of 2009, which was a huge deal for him because he was baptized in front of hundreds of people despite his fear and anxiety. Dripping wet and beaming, he sought me out in the crowd and told me this day was one of the most important days of his life.

"This is why we opened the Karis House doors — to serve this guy and the thousands like him in our city."

Conclusion

All of the ministries mentioned here have several important things in common. Yes, they are all successful in their own areas, and yes, they have moved out from the umbrella of the church in order to be self-sustaining organizations that partner with churches and community organizations all over the city. And yes, Josh, James, and Joel all start with the letter J!

But the most important shared traits of these three organizations are more fundamental than that.

Each began with a Journey intern or staff member listening for God's direction, not just for the purpose of finding a nontraditional church job. James, Josh, and Joel wanted God to give them a calling for life and to see their ministry work as more than just a job.

None of these men waited for "the church" to advance their agenda. These men didn't see The Journey as yet another church that was failing to specialize in their areas of interest. Instead of leaving the church because we didn't offer their pet program, they *stayed* at the church precisely because we didn't offer their pet program! They knew that if The Journey was going to truly serve St. Louis, they needed to roll up their sleeves, take bold risks, and lead the charge into uncharted territory.

Each of these ministries began with leaders taking years to assess authentically the needs of the people they were called to serve. They were not trying to mimic the ministry of a church in New York or California or London. While all three organizations learned from churches and businesses all over the country in the process of setting up shop, the primary work they did that has made them successful was to look deep into the lives of people in St. Louis and see how the gospel could address the needs exposed in their searching.

Each ministry started out only slightly better than a disaster. Before words like "success" and "accomplishments" came words and phrases like "unfocused," "no strategy," "scattered," "stuck," and "disillusioned." But instead of folding up the tents or settling for less than what they could be, these leaders acknowledged their weaknesses, prayed for clarity, and listened to those who could help them succeed.

As we close this chapter on service I want to leave you with some questions to help you determine if you are doing all you can to assess and meet the needs of your city so you can serve the people who live there.[5]

- Whom has God called you (your church) to serve? Is it young families, senior citizens, employees of local restaurants, recent high school dropouts, a particular ethnic group, or single men and women? Try to be specific here. Serving "the poor" sounds noble, but what does it really mean? How do you define "poor"? Do you mean homeless men and women? Do you mean the underemployed? Drill down into specifics so that your service will be more focused, sustainable, and effective.
- What are the five most pressing needs of that group? Think holistically and practically when answering this question. For example, what do people need spiritually, financially, emotionally, physically, and the like?
- What do you currently possess that would be beneficial to others? This could be a particular skill, disposable income, a flexible schedule, or a wide variety of other things.
- What do your friends and family members currently possess that would be beneficial to the group you have been called to serve?
- Where is God already working, and how can you join him in his restorative, healing ministry?
- Where are the people you are called to serve gathering?
- Where are the people you are called to serve finding their sense of identity or purpose?
- How does the gospel address the needs of the group you are called to serve? If the group was to define "good news," what would the definition look like?

---

5. These questions are inspired by questions found in Alan Hirsch and Darryn Altclass, *The Forgotten Ways Handbook* (Grand Rapids: Brazos, 2009), 99.

CHAPTER 7

Equipping
(Matt)

How can my church be *different?*" That's the question I most often hear when I share the story of The Austin Stone with other people. They want to know *how* we became the church we are today, a church *for* the city of Austin. And that's a good question. It's the right question to be asking right now.

When I think about the story God has been writing through our church, I start by remembering that this was all his doing—his plan long before the foundation of the world and certainly before I ever came on the scene. But there was a starting point for me, a sabbatical where God spoke and where the vision began coming together. I had spent hours poring over the Word, studying Scriptures such as Isaiah 58 and Matthew 25, when God suddenly made it clear that if we wanted to be his church *for* the city, things had to change.

We could no longer play it safe and stay on the sidelines.

I sensed that God wanted to bend the heart of our church toward the poor and the afflicted. He was asking us to get our hands dirty and do the very things we had avoided doing. But his calling was clear. For me, following this vision, this call out of the comfortable life I had been living, was as sure to me as breathing air. It felt as if it was something I had to do, whatever the cost, because the cost of ignoring it would be even higher. I decided then and there that even if every person I knew thought I was crazy, I was going to follow what God was asking me. I remember saying to God, "If you want me to go, I'll go."

But I also felt as if God's message to our church was a warning. I sensed that God was fighting for our hearts, that he was unwilling to let us sit around and "play" church, only to realize that we had completely missed his will. Nothing makes my stomach turn over more than the thought of missing out on the wonderful things God had planned because I was too comfortable with the status quo. God's challenge to me and to our church was further evidence of his grace. He was resolutely committed to changing us into people who care about the things and the people he cares about.

Still, there were many people who weren't on that mountainside with me, who didn't hear the call from God and weren't convinced. I knew what God wanted us to do—the church he wanted us to become—but how was I going to translate this countercultural call to the six thousand people who called The Austin Stone their church?

Casting a Vision

When I returned from my sabbatical, I remember specifically praying that God would ignite the heart of each person at our church in the same way he had touched mine. I begged for God to pour out his Spirit and fill our church so that people were ready and willing to embrace a new vision for ministry. I knew that if our city was ever going to change, we had to take responsibility for the problems and needs facing Austin, and to do that we were going to have to get our people on board. I began preaching a vision series following my sabbatical, and it became one of the most empowering and decisive seasons in our church's history.

It wasn't because I had suddenly become the most persuasive preacher. Rather, God began to move in unprecedented ways in our body. By his grace, our people were hungry to grow and change. If you are a pastor or a church leader, you probably know what I'm talking about. Our people were tired of just showing up on Sundays, serving once a month and calling that a "church." As I cast the vision for something bigger, something rooted in the heart that God had for the people of Austin, it felt as if God was waking a sleeping giant. I learned that our people were just as ready as I was to live out the gospel they saw in the Bible.

As I talked with people, I heard that they longed to make the transition from spectator Christianity into the kind of gospel movement that could change a city—a movement that God could use to change the world. And I should add that this was more than a passing interest in social justice. Our church saw this as an opportunity to join ranks with those working to fulfill the Great Commission. They began to see that it was no longer necessary to cross an ocean to become a missionary. Instead, God was calling them to cross the highway and minister on the street corners of some of the toughest neighborhoods in Austin. We were confident that Austin would soon feel the redemptive presence of God's people.

Mobilization: Missional Community

While this prophetic shift was taking shape, awakening the hearts of our people with fresh vision and teaching from the Scriptures, there were also some changes occurring within our existing structure and ministry philosophy that made it possible for us to execute the vision.

First, we began to shift from seeing church as a destination to seeing it as an identity. Instead of thinking that we *went* to church, we began to emphasize the biblical teaching that we *are* the church. As simple as this may sound, it took awhile for our people to understand and embrace this fundamental truth. Now, our people believe this with deep conviction, and it is one of the blessings that I am most thankful for as a pastor. Because our people immediately see themselves as the church, our representation of Christ in the community goes far beyond our Sunday worship services.

Second, we began investigating a new structure for relating to each other and to our neighborhoods, something we called *missional communities*. We began moving away from a traditional small group model that emphasized church community and evangelism by invitation. While this model continues to be popular at many churches, we saw several barriers in this model that kept us from truly engaging the people of the city who were not from a church background. The very people who needed to hear the gospel weren't able to establish relationships with those who were sharing the gospel.

Existing small group models typically aim for community first, but they often miss the mark and are ineffective at fostering either mission *or* community. Yet when they aim for *mission* first, they are effective at fostering mission *and* developing organic forms of community. When community was the focus, mission and community both suffered. But when mission takes priority, community naturally follows.

Interesting.

We decided that since disciple-making is best done by missionaries who are living out the Great Commission to specific people, we needed to redefine the identity of our community leaders, seeing them us missionaries rather than small group leaders. We also encountered several problems with our existing small group model as a vehicle for reaching the city. For example, a core quality of a missionary is that they embrace a cross-centered identity and have a readiness to lose everything for the sake of sharing the gospel with lost people. That means that they willingly forgo things that they love, things that make them comfortable, things that are part of their daily life, for the sake of reaching lost people—incarnating themselves into another subculture or group of people to share the gospel of Jesus.

But how do evangelical believers accustomed to a spectator model of worship transition from low commitment to high commitment? From inwardly focused small groups into missional communities? Answer: you just do it! You *act* your way into a new way of thinking. This is a relational process, not a one-time announcement. We have learned that casting a vision isn't enough to inspire spectator Christians to become missional believers. Why? Because spectator Christians will simply accommodate the missional vision to their preexisting categories. They'll add the right lingo but *never change their behavior.* They will embrace the vision but never change the way they live.

That's why you have to:

1. Act
2. Repeatedly
3. Over time

You must act repeatedly over time to become different. It takes all three of these factors working together in concert. The habits, dispositions, and sensibilities of spectator Christianity don't change overnight. Leadership development happens little by little, topic by topic, over time. The goal is not just picking up the right lingo or being able to state the vision clearly; it's a passion to see behaviors and lifestyles really change.

You see, missional communities are not simply an *arm* of our church. They *are* our church. They are core to our identity. Take them away, and we are no longer a church. These are communities of Christ followers on mission with God, following the Holy Spirit, while demonstrating and declaring the gospel of Jesus Christ to a specific pocket of people. We aren't waiting for the lost to come to us; we go to them. We want to tear down the false teaching that has crept into our churches that church is all about checking an attendance box and eating out after service on Sundays. We want to replace it with an understanding that the church is a group of radically changed people infiltrating the world and propelled to love others at great cost to themselves, all empowered by the simple message of the gospel.

Still, after all that I've just written, you might still be wondering to yourself: *Aren't these just glorified small groups? If not, how exactly are your missional communities different from an evangelistically focused small group? Isn't your missional community label just flavor-of-the-month jargon for the small groups that just about every church has?*

That's a fair question. The small group movement took off several decades ago, and as we have studied the movement and its development and reflected on our own experience, we have found that small groups seem to be characterized by a different identity. Our missional communities are characterized by two key qualities.

First, missional communities are committed to intentionally spending time with the pocket of people with whom God has placed them. Those who commit to a community don't just leave the people they are with and look for others to serve; rather, they serve right where they are. They engage the people around them with the Word of God and regularly declare the gospel through their lifestyle, their conversations, and prayers for people.

Notice the shift of focus here. These are not communities that exist to provide fellowship among believers or to help people feel more connected. Certainly, we value those things as well, but we believe that they will develop naturally in communities that are primarily focusing on the mission of Christ. Our primary focus is external, not the internal needs of the church. And as that mission is mutually engaged by each member of the community, it will gradually extinguish any traces of consumerism (a self-centered satisfaction of our own needs) that might keep us from experiencing true community. Missional communities are structured and defined so that they focus on identifying the needs of their neighbors, serving them as a demonstration of the gospel.

Second, missional communities must multiply. We believe our ability to reach the city is directly connected to the growth and spread of our missional DNA. If we have groups that are intentionally pushing the brakes so that they don't multiply, we aren't effectively spreading the message. A missional community is not merely a smaller component of the larger group; a missional community is more like a stem cell, a cell that can continue to reproduce in a variety of different ways and continue reproducing. Missional communities contain the DNA of the larger group with a strong imperative to replicate.

With small groups, we've found that some groups will grow, while others don't. Some small groups become holy huddles for years on end, with fellowship as the end-all, be-all of the group.

They aren't focused on reproducing; they are focused on care, study, and the development of long-term relationships.

Missional communities, by contrast, are DNA-carriers of the larger body, and they replicate that DNA wherever they exist. To switch analogies, missional communities are like bifocal lenses: they balance the *internal* focus of following Jesus with an *external* focus on incarnating the gospel in the community. As such, missional communities are better suited for doing contextualized replication of the church body. To put it simply, a missional community is ready to be a new church plant. We are ready to send a missional community out to be a separate church if the occasion calls for it.

Yes, you read that right; we are ready to let go of our communities and see them become separate churches. Missional communities are our agents for this replication; and they must have a core identity that embraces a commitment to multiply and share the gospel with people from the city. The gospel must be spread virally.

Once we had this infrastructure in place and began mobilizing our people and connecting them to the needs of lost people in Austin, God began using us to promote the welfare of our city. We were convinced that the shalom of Austin, Texas, was going to be built on the backs of our missional communities.

Catalyzing: The For the City Center (FTCC)

So you've got the vision and now you're ready to jump in and get started, right? But *how*? What do you actually do to catalyze movement? Even though I'd preached an inspirational series and we had restructured our small group communities, we still weren't sure how to begin practically implementing this vision. We saw there were organizations all around us that were working hard to improve and restore the broken parts of Austin, but we also realized there was something missing in their efforts. These were all individual teams working in isolation from one another, and they lacked unity.

That's when we realized we'd forgotten a key piece of the puzzle.

Our vision to seek the well-being of our city was nothing new. For a younger generation growing up in a culture that emphasizes individualism and breeds a consumer mentality, it might have seemed radical and new, but there was a time not too long ago when entire communities and churches would gather together and work with one another for the common good of the city.

In fact, as we looked at the history of larger cities, we found evidence of this in the way they were laid out and designed. Older towns once had a town square that operated as the functional center of the city. It was surrounded by the institutions of commerce and trade, law and government, the arts and places for dialogue. But alongside these key cultural institutions was always the church. The entire city would be situated around a center, and that's what tied life in the city together. Again, the church was always an integral part of that connection.

So we wondered: Was it possible to give new life to that long-lost vision of connection and unity, where multiple institutions came together for the common good of the city? Could it happen once again? What if there was once again a *center* that tied the city together? What could we, as a church, do to nurture that kind of connection for the benefit of Austin?

Don't Reinvent the Wheel

As we thought about this concept of a central connection place for city renewal, we began brainstorming all sorts of exciting possibilities. Then we hit the pause button again. We wanted to make this dream a reality, but we began to see a potential landmine as well, one that we wanted to avoid at all costs. We didn't want to be the "Great White Church" riding in to fix problems from the outside, problems that we barely understood.

We saw there were plenty of great organizations already knee-deep in serving the city of Austin; they just weren't working together. Could we come alongside those who were already serving and accelerate their impact on the city? What if we could foster, by offering physical space at our church building, a center for collaboration between the various organizations that were already serving the city? Could we bless the people already at work and help them come together in a unifying way?

We didn't need to reinvent the wheel. Since there were already seasoned organizations with a mature understanding of how to best meet the needs of the city, we didn't need to take the people of our church and start lots of new ministries. Rather than learn all of the detailed and somewhat technical competencies necessary to start and maintain dozens of new nonprofits, couldn't we just flood the existing organizations with people? People with new hearts and a passion to volunteer and love others?

We decided that the people of The Austin Stone would become a church for the city through the work of dozens of well-functioning nonprofit ministries. We didn't have to go and start something new. We could serve anywhere in the city within the unique channel of an already established nonprofit ministry.

Meanwhile ...

While all of these conversations were happening, our church also experienced a major shift in our future plans for physical space, plans we had made to house our growing church. We had two options: search for a building that could be renovated or find some land and build. We knew that building was the more difficult option, since getting land and constructing a facility would likely cost us tens of millions of dollars.

Now, I've been around churches long enough to know that one of the greatest roadblocks to engaging in the mission of God is debt. So when I heard people quoting some of the numbers and the cost of building, I knew that taking on this level of debt would likely have a significant impact on our ability to minister to the city. One of our pastors shared with me his sense that if we built a new building, it would be the *only* major project our church would be able to take on for the next seven years.

Seven years?

I began to picture the chokehold that debt like that could have on us. And I knew that I didn't want to bury our church under that kind of load, especially if there was another way.

The Broader Scope of Multisite

Instead of growing discouraged, though, these obstacles motivated us to think outside the box. We knew that it would be nice to have a large auditorium that could hold large numbers of people, a facility that would meet our capacity need in one location. It seemed more efficient—even easier in some ways—to have everyone in one place. But it wasn't our only option, and we weren't sure that it was really the best way to align with our missional call. After all, having people drive from the four corners of the city to worship in one location made things easier for *us*, but was that really the best way to reach the people?

It began to sound like yet another way of getting people to bend over backward just to come to our facility. To effectively minister to the needs of people, we decided to search for another location in an entirely new part of the city, a place where we could establish yet another faithful presence in Austin. We would keep meeting at the high school where we currently met, but we would begin multiplying our presence through multiple sites around the city of Austin.

Land, Ho!

You may recall that I received a phone call during my sabbatical about a piece of land that was for sale in a forgotten, impoverished, and abandoned part of Austin. I haven't really painted the picture clearly enough for you. You may have an image in your mind and think I'm talking about a rough place. But to describe it more accurately, the land was *ruined*. After praying and seeking the

Lord, we made the decision to move ahead and purchase the land, but we first needed to have it professionally cleaned. Yes, cleaned. To help us with this, we solicited the services of three separate companies who specialized in clearing land of trash, debris, and waste. Before any of these companies would take on a job, however, they first needed to visit the site and give us an estimate of the cost. Three companies came to look over the site. Two of them refused even to give us a bid.

The land was a wasteland of broken needles, soiled mattresses, and used condoms. Of course, these things were indicators of the regular, daily activities that had been happening on the land for years. The company that agreed to help us clear the land eventually filled two dump trucks and another *twelve* pickup trucks worth of debris.

And they did it all while wearing hazmat suits.

The St. John neighborhood of Austin has both the highest crime rate and the lowest high school graduation rate within the city. Teen pregnancy and violence are all too common for the children growing up in the neighborhood. If ever there was a neighborhood in Austin that needed someone to seek God on its behalf, this was it.

It wasn't our first choice for a property, but we could sense that God was going to use us to redeem the land. We also knew that God was doing more than changing the neighborhood ... he was changing our hearts as well. He was teaching us to see things and value people as he did. We were humbled to realize that not only was this an opportunity for us to show the world the love of God through his church, we the church would be transformed in the process.

There was a large facility on the property, and immediately we began considering how we could best use the facility for our Sunday worship gatherings. Then we began to think about the rest of the week. What if the building was being used Monday through Saturday as well? Could this property create an opportunity for us to unite our vision for space with our vision for mission? Was this the "center" we had been praying for?

Facilitating: The For the City Network (FTCN)

We decided to open our facility during the week and began inviting various organizations and nonprofits that were already working in the city to use our building. We wanted this location to be more than just a church campus. We wanted it branded as a space for nonprofits that were serving the people and the neighborhoods of Austin, a hub for collaboration that happened to house a group of people for worship on Sundays.

So far, God had provided everything we needed: the vision, the church of people, the money, the land, and the space. It was time to move this center of synergy from theory into reality. All that was left was to fill this center with organizations and nonprofits that were already serving the city with excellence. Yes, our church would meet there on Sunday, but the building wasn't our church. Our church would be out with our ministry partners, Monday through Saturday, serving the needs of the city.

Early on we made a strategic decision that the organizations that occupied our building did *not* necessarily have to be faith-based organizations. They might not all share our church's mission of redemption in Christ for the joy of all peoples. However, we did require that each organization housed in our center at least be sympathetic with our biblical vision. While they didn't need to fully embrace our biblical vision as a church, the organization couldn't be *anti*-biblical in its beliefs and practices. If the organizations supported our biblical mission, that was great; but we decided that we could still work with them and partner with them even if they were silent or neutral about our biblical principles. But if an organization was actively working or speaking out against our biblical mission, we would not partner with them.

The sad truth is that in many places in America, the church has been sleeping for quite some time. The experts on meeting the needs of impoverished and underserved people are frequently not the people in our churches. Secular organizations have also been in the business of serving people in need for some time now, and many of them are actually pretty good at it. If we desire to serve the city in the best way possible, then churches may have to walk a humble path and admit that there are people out there already doing the work better than we can … and that's okay. We all want some of the same things: our streets restored and our city to thrive. It's not the faith commitment of the organization that matters most. It's the faith commitment of the people working in those organizations, the hands and feet that are out there serving each and every day. And that's where we invest our resources.

Another sad reality is that some of those with the greatest needs have been neglected by the church and want nothing to do with it. They trust the nonprofit sector and feel safe having their needs met by them rather than the church. Some of this is due to our own self-centeredness and lack of care. Collectively, as a church, we've been ignoring needs and hoarding blessings. Even if their reasons for rejecting help from the church are irrational or unwarranted, the Bible is still clear that we are supposed to *go to them*, not the other way around.

Again, let me reiterate that we do not engage partnerships with organizations and nonprofits that stand against the gospel of Jesus Christ. Our vision for all of this is to maximize our efforts to renew Austin by creating a funnel for volunteer engagement, an emphasis on identifying needs, and a platform for facilitating strategic partnerships. To this end, we launched The For the City Network as an official 501(c)3 nonprofit in January 2009 and The For the City Center in September 2010.[1] Our initial hope, during Phase One, was to lease out some of our space to some of the different partners in The For the City Network.

But that didn't happen.

Instead, we had leased out *all* of our space! Our tenants and partners in the center are four of the strongest nonprofits in Austin, doing some of the best volunteer work in the city their area of specialty. The four tenants for the facility are Communities In Schools, Capital Area Food Bank, Caring Family Network, and

---

1. For more information on the For the City Network, please visit www.forthecity.org and follow the latest stories of how God is changing the city of Austin.

Austin LifeGuard. Let me give you a quick sketch of these ministries and share how each of these organizations, as partners of The For the City Network, are working to serve the city of Austin.

Communities In Schools (CIS)

CIS and their ASPIRE Literacy Program was our anchor tenant. ASPIRE (Achieving Success through Parental Involvement, Reading, and Education) strives to break the cycle of illiteracy and poverty in families by providing comprehensive, integrated literacy services for the entire family. CIS works to encourage education "from the cradle to college." ASPIRE includes early childhood education, adult education, parenting classes, and in-home tutoring. In short, ASPIRE helps raise the levels of education children are receiving while providing resources and confidence for parents of young children. They encourage and equip parents to lead their families well.

Capital Area Food Bank (CAFB)

Currently, CAFB is the second-largest food bank in the country and provides food and grocery products to 350 food pantries in 21 counties in Central Texas. They will be sponsoring and running a model food pantry in the east wing of The For the City Center. This pantry will be one of only three food-bank-run food pantries in Central Texas and is designed to serve as a model for not just our city's but for our nation's food banks. In addition to providing relief in times of crisis, CAFB will begin to offer development opportunities to their clients to help them move toward personal sustainability and away from day-to-day food needs.

Caring Family Network (CFN)

Adoption and foster care are close to the heart of The Austin Stone, and our partnership with Caring Family Network is a perfect match. CFN's mission is to connect children, families, and communities. CFN trains prospective foster parents and families preparing for adoption, cares for traumatized, abused, and neglected children, and much more.

Austin LifeGuard

Austin LifeGuard, a program of Austin LifeCare—a pregnancy resource center—focuses on abstinence-based sex education. LifeGuard's mission is to work to empower teens in the Austin-area with accurate information and practical tools to help them make healthy decisions, build strong relationships, and fully experience the benefits of saving sex for marriage.

One of the most exciting fruits of having these organizations housed under the same roof has been watching new relationships form and seeing new opportunities for collaboration materialize. For instance, Capitol Area Food Bank decided when they moved in that they wanted to go beyond handing out food to those in need and begin offering restorative services and training to help people get off the food line permanently. They knew they needed to add a case management structure to their existing business model—but they had no idea how to do this! Just down the hallway, though, is Caring Family Network, whose *specialty* happens to be case management. Through their connection at The For the City Center, these two nonprofits have begun to work together to mutually support their respective efforts to serve the city.

The Fruit of Partnership

This was exactly what we had hoped for in networking with these nonprofits: synergy for the collective good of Austin. Our network now has additional partners who serve all across Austin, in addition to the four that are currently housed within The For the City Center, and every week we are finding new ways of working together for the good of the city.

For instance, instead of starting new mentoring or tutoring programs, The For the City Network now partners with Big Brothers/ Big Sisters (one of the largest and most respected mentoring organizations in the country) and several local schools in our neighborhood to provide mentors to children and adolescents. At Reagan High School, which is within the St. John Community, we partner with the school administration and the various nonprofits that work within the school to empower volunteers, many of whom are part of the missional communities of The Austin Stone. This combined effort has thus far deployed over six hundred individuals to serve, mentor, and love the students of these under-resourced neighborhood schools over the past two years.

We are also seeing thousands of people in our church being exposed to parts of the city they would have never visited before. As they overcome fear and the discomfort of leaving behind safe comfort zones, the church is loving people with the gospel, people whom they would never have come into contact otherwise.

And the crazy thing about all of this is that it's actually making a difference.

The Reagan High School students who have been blessed by tutors, mentors, and coaches through FTCN have shown remarkable signs of development over the past two years. Last year, the same leaders who had been training these teenagers in life skills and Christian discipleship took fourteen students to Kibera, in Nairobi, Kenya, one of the largest, most densely populated slums in the world. The students raised thousands of dollars to go overseas and serve abandoned and forgotten children living in another nation. Experiences like that change people, and we are beginning to see the power of the gospel through this work.

At the end of the day, though, this is not just about "volunteering" to serve our city and help people — it's about incarnation. It's about giving our lives for the sake of those in need to share the message of hope that we have found in Jesus Christ. And we do this by serving.

What's Next?

The Lord stirred the heart of our church several years ago and led us to study Isaiah 58, focusing on verse 12:

And your ancient ruins shall be rebuilt;
     you shall raise up the foundations of many generations;

you shall be called the repairer of the breach,
the restorer of streets to dwell in.

This verse challenged us to ask ourselves two questions: Will we ever be considered, in Austin, the "restorer of the streets"? Are we living and loving and serving in such a way that becoming "the restorer of streets" is our trajectory, our goal?

What have we seen since that time?

The Lord has blessed us with a new property in the St. John neighborhood. And *already* we have seen that our presence there—not just our talents—in this neighborhood has become a catalyst for change. *Already* over fifty people from The Austin Stone have moved into the neighborhood as listeners, learners, and neighbors, but mostly as missionaries. They have done this after selling everything and leaving behind comfortable, "safe" lifestyles, forsaking it all to know Christ and share in his mission. The tide is turning in this area of the city.

Schools that were literally days from being shut down by the Texas Education Agency have now been upgraded to a higher academic status through the work of committed followers of Christ serving students, teachers, and administrators. Many students are now impacting their schools for the gospel by declaring the message of Jesus to their friends and teachers.

Partnerships are already developing among a number of churches in the city to help address the growing number of orphans living in foster care in Austin. Collaboration is helping each child find a home and is providing a living testimony to the gospel. We are working to help each child find an adopted family, a reminder that we ourselves were once adopted into the family of God.

This chapter started with the question: "How can my church be different?" I hope you now hear the answer to that question. God has given us his Word and his life so that we can know his heart. We know *how* to be a church that looks like him—it's no mystery! We follow Jesus and refuse to allow our hearts to serve idols of comfort and security. We embrace the visions of the living God, who is on the move in the midst of our cities.

God is not asleep, nor is he dead. He is alive today, and he is calling you to join him.

God has invited you, as part of his church, to join him in redeeming and restoring a world broken by the effects of sin. The only question now is: *Will you go?*

CHAPTER 8

Suffering (Matt)

Therefore let those who suffer according to God's will entrust their souls to a faithful Creator while doing good.

1 PETER 4:19

Count it all joy, my brothers, when you meet trials of various kinds, for you know that the testing of your faith produces steadfastness.

JAMES 1:2–3

When I was getting the results of my church planting assessment, the major concern my assessors had about my potential to plant successfully had nothing to do with my theology, or preaching, or rugged good looks. In fact, the assessors praised and encouraged me on nearly every front. Except one.

"There's one thing I'm worried about," said the lead assessor. "Matt, you've never suffered."

He was right.

At that point in my life, the only person who had died in my family was my sweet ninety-six-year-old great-grandmother, who died in her sleep after loving Jesus her whole life. Everyone else was still alive. There was no sickness. No poverty. No great tragedy. Which meant, for me, little understanding of what it meant to suffer.

The assessor said, "Matt, I think you're going to have trouble relating to people on the deepest levels because you haven't experienced the kind of suffering they'll be bringing with them into your church."

I knew my Bible well enough to know that suffering is a constant theme in the Scriptures. And I knew my life well enough to know that the assessors were right. I hadn't really suffered much, at least not on a level that would allow me to empathize with seriously wounded people in need of a gospel conversation with someone who, like them, had been through hell and back.

I guess God really wanted me to plant The Stone, because he immediately put into motion a plan to fortify my primary area of weakness as a church planter—my lack of experience in suffering. Three months after I took the assessment, my fifty-seven-year-old mother died unexpectedly. At the time, I was twenty-seven years old. Not long after that, my dad was diagnosed with an aortic aneurysm, had open-heart surgery, and was given a few years to live.

If all of that wasn't personal enough, I was diagnosed with cancer.

Needless to say, God immediately had my attention, and to use C. S. Lewis's phrase, I felt as if he was shouting at me through the megaphone of suffering.[1] Not only was I better qualified to plant a church, but I began to feel as if I was now a member of the great cloud of witnesses who have shown the glory of God through the medium of their faithful suffering.

Not "If" but "When"

The Bible promises us many things. Here are just a few:

- Eternal life for those who have faith in Jesus—1 John 2:25
- A new heart, right desires, and a new spirit of love—Ezekiel 36:26
- Forgiveness from sin—1 John 1:9
- Deliverance from fear—Psalm 34:4
- Provision for all needs—Philippians 4:19
- Peace with God and others—Isaiah 26:3; Romans 5:1

---

1. The exact quote is, "God whispers to us in our pleasures, speaks in our conscience, but shouts in our pain: it is His megaphone to rouse a deaf world" (C. S. Lewis, *The Problem of Pain* [New York: HarperCollins, 2001], 91).

What's even better than any of these, though, is the promise that God actually *keeps* all his promises, and Jesus Christ is our guarantee: "For all the promises of God find their Yes in him. That is why it is through him that we utter our Amen to God for his glory" (2 Cor. 1:20). This is good news for God's people. When God promises something, we can take it to the bank.

That is certainly an encouraging word. But the promises of God begin to lose a little of their luster when we consider the fact that God also promises us the very thing that we spend most of our lives trying to avoid: *suffering.* Yes, God promises us suffering—suffering for both the Christian and the non-Christian.

The prophet Isaiah was one of the people who had the unfortunate calling to share this unpopular message. In Isaiah 43:2, God speaks through Isaiah:

> When you pass through the waters, I will be with you;
>   and through the rivers, they shall not overwhelm you;
> when you walk through fire you shall not be burned,
>   and the flame shall not consume you.

Though this may sound comforting at first glance, notice what God doesn't say in this verse, "*If* you happen to stumble upon a trial," or "*If* you belong to me you won't suffer." No, God says to us, "*When* you suffer...." Belonging to Jesus, going to church, helping old ladies across the street ... none of this is going to spare you or me from suffering. Why? Because God has promised suffering. He has promised us that we will suffer for his glory and for our own good.

There is something unique about the experience of suffering that brings God glory and actually benefits us. Isaiah is not the only place in the Bible where we learn about suffering. In fact, a passage in 1 Peter helps us unpack some of the reasons why suffering is actually a good thing in the life of a follower of Christ. Peter helps us better understand some of God's purposes in our suffering.

Peter wrote to a community of suffering Christians in order to help them gain perspective as they went through trials and difficult times. Early in the letter, Peter writes, "Now for a little while, if necessary, you have been grieved by various trials, so that the tested genuineness of your faith—more precious than gold that perishes though it is tested by fire—may be found to result in praise and glory and honor at the revelation of Jesus Christ" (1 Peter 1:6–7). Peter tells the church that suffering well brings good things to us as Christians. Suffering tests the most precious gift we have been given—faith—and reminds us that God's gift has eternal benefits that are strengthened and refined by our suffering.

Of particular significance is Peter's reference to a refining fire. You may remember that Isaiah spoke about suffering as a "walk through the fire" as well. What is significant about the image of fire here? Fire has been used for centuries to refine and remove impurities and imperfections, particularly for metals. Peter likens our trouble and pain and suffering to a refining fire, and in so doing he may have been thinking of the story about Daniel's three friends, who were thrown into a fiery furnace in Daniel 3.

In case you don't remember the story, here's the CliffsNotes version. Daniel's three friends refused to bow down in worship to the statue of King Nebuchadnezzar, the pagan king at the time. In anger, King Nebby tossed the three young men into a super-heated furnace (heated seven times hotter than usual, according to Dan. 3:19). The fire was so hot that some of the men who threw Shadrach, Meshach, and Abednego into the furnace were killed!

Eager to see the rebels meet their end, Nebby looked into the furnace; but instead of seeing three melting Jews, he saw four perfectly healthy men walking around in the furnace, with the fourth man being "like a son of the gods" (Dan. 3:25). And who was the fourth man? Well, we now believe that this fourth man was Jesus. In what theologians call a "Christophany," a physical appearance of Christ before the incarnation, we see a fulfillment of the promise God gave to his people in Isaiah 43:2. In the story of Daniel's friends, God was *literally* with his people in the midst of a fiery trial, and they made it through OK. They didn't die. They weren't utterly consumed. They didn't melt away. When God's people needed protection from the heat, God showed up. They survived the trial, and their survival drew King Nebuchadnezzar's full attention to "the God of Shadrach, Meshach, and Abednego" (Dan. 3:28).

One of the most important things we as the church can show to our cities and our neighbors is how Christians suffer well, to the glory of God. After all, nothing grabs the attention of unbelievers like suffering. And when we suffer in a way that is different, when we suffer with an abiding faith and trust in God, it makes a statement to those who are watching.

Suffering: The Evangelist's Secret Weapon

The greatest evangelism technique of the first and second century church was not the Four Spiritual Laws or a Billy Graham Crusade. Surprisingly, it wasn't even going door-to-door with gospel tracts. No, the most effective tool for reaching non-Christians in the days of the early church was the pain reflex of the church. And there was plenty of pain. Christians were subjected to some of the most horrible, torturous kinds of physical pain. In some cases, it was the kind of pain that would tempt most of us to curse God and our spouse, kids, and friends. Several stunning acts of violence were committed against late-first-century Christians under the Roman emperors Nero and Domitian.[2]

- Christians were thrown to wild animals to be torn apart while crowds of thousands watched and cheered the mauling.
- While still alive, Christians were covered with pitch and set on fire to provide lighting for nightly parties at Nero's gardens.
- Christians were crucified by the hundreds and sometimes thousands along the main highways in and out of Rome as

---

2. First-century Roman historian Cornelius Tacitus (AD 55–120) recorded the following regarding the persecution of Christians under Nero (*Annals* 15.44). "Covered with the skins of beasts, [Christians] were torn by dogs and perished, or were nailed to crosses, or were doomed to the flames and burnt, to serve as a nightly illumination, when daylight had expired."

a lesson to all those observers who might desire to claim a lord other than the emperor.

So, how did the experience of unbearable physical suffering contribute to the explosive growth of the early church? Again, it was not the pain of suffering that led to growth; it was the church's pain reflex—the way these Christians *responded* to their suffering.

Christians who paid the ultimate price and died for their persecution were called martyrs. The word *martyr* comes from the Greek word *martys*, meaning "witness." While some of those who were killed for their faith may have been literal witnesses of Christ's resurrection and ascension, those in later years were witnesses of a different sort—witnesses to the goodness and grace of God. And their faithfulness to the gospel and their love for Jesus was a witness to the watching world. Justin Martyr, a Christian killed for his faith around AD 165, was severely beaten, nearly to the point of death, and given one last chance for reprieve if he would only denounce the lordship of Christ. He responded, "We Christians desire nothing more than to suffer for our Lord Jesus Christ."

He was beheaded moments later.

The reports from historians of the time tell other stories similar to Justin's. Polycarp was an early church leader who was willing to be burned alive, telling his executioners that they didn't even need to fasten him to the stake, for his faith in Christ would keep him there. Other stories capture scenes of Christians singing hymns of joy while being killed and torn apart by wild animals before crowds of thousands.

These believers were witnesses—martyrs—to the gospel of God's grace by the way they responded to their intense suffering. They suffered in a way that caught the eyes, ears, and imagination of the nonbelieving world. What strength, what power did these people have that allowed them to endure such suffering? The answer, of course, is Jesus, the Lord of heaven and earth, the one who suffered the brutality of the Roman cross uttering, "Father, forgive them for they know not what they do" (Luke 23:34). The strength they had is the same strength we need to respond rightly to suffering, and it is found in the person and work of Jesus.

At the cross, we see God's willingness to suffer *with* and *for* his people. As one of us, Jesus knew the pain of deep emotional, psychological, and physical suffering. Suffering was not a theory or mere theological belief for him; it was a matter of life and death, and it was very real. Jesus is presently able to be *with* us in our suffering because he was one of us as he suffered.

But at the cross we also see that Jesus suffered *for* us, "on our behalf." As the perfect representative of Adam's race, his death was sacrificial, a death died not to atone for his own sin but for the sins of the world. Not only did Jesus suffer, he suffered well. As the writer of Hebrews says, "For it was fitting that he, for whom and by whom all things exist, in bringing many sons to glory, should make the founder of their salvation perfect through suffering" (Heb. 2:10). Many people have been brought to glory, to eternal life, through the perfect suffering of Jesus. Our Lord is "Jesus the Sufferer." In fact, Jesus is Lord, the author of Hebrews tells us, *because* he suffered. The King of glory, who reigns victorious, is a fitting king for us because he is also the Lamb of God who was led to the slaughter.

Suffering like Jesus

The Bible says that Jesus is our model for how to suffer well: "Since therefore Christ suffered in the flesh, arm yourselves with the same way of thinking, for whoever has suffered in the flesh has ceased from sin, so as to live for the rest of the time in the flesh no longer for human passions but for the will of God" (1 Peter 4:1–2). Suffering provides an opportunity for us to learn what it means to be true disciples of Jesus, to surrender our whole lives to God, even (and especially) in the very worst and most difficult moments of our lives.

In Matthew 16:24, Jesus clarified to his disciples exactly what it meant to be his follower: "If anyone would come after me, let him deny himself and take up his cross and follow me." As we now know, taking up the cross was more than a symbol or metaphor for Jesus. It was his vocation, his reason for becoming incarnate! And when Jesus called his disciples to follow him, he was not suggesting that they grin and bear a burden or two here or there. He was, and still is today, calling people to trust him and witness to his sacrificial love in the most painful, shameful times of our lives. "Enter boldly and faithfully into your God-appointed suffering. The world is watching! Let them *see* you follow me," he says to each of us.

As we close out our look at the biblical call to suffer for Christ and the gospel, I want to share some real-time stories of suffering that we have experienced in our community. One of the stories highlights how we can respond to personal suffering and see God's goodness in it. The other is an example of how we can respond to the suffering of others and encourage them to see God's goodness in it.

As you read these stories, keep in mind that of all the things the church can do, there is not much that we can do better than the world. But the church can suffer in a way that is unique. Suffering well is something the church can model for the rest of the world. We can be witnesses to God and his gospel as we suffer. The church, if it loves its city, will teach and model the importance of suffering well. As we suffer with and for our city, we suffer like Christ—sacrificially, pointing others to the goodness of God, for his glory.

Suffering with People

One of the neighborhoods God has called The Stone to reach for Christ is the St. Johns neighborhood. In 2009, a twenty-four-unit apartment complex in the neighborhood caught fire and was destroyed in a matter of minutes. Most of those living there were under-resourced; many were single moms, and some were immigrants. Everyone lost everything they owned but the clothes they had on at the time.

A partner at The Stone found out about the fire as it was happening. Through Twitter, Facebook, and numerous phone calls, he mobilized our church so that within thirty minutes we had hundreds of folks on the ground, working with the Red Cross to find out what people needed. Within five hours, The Stone had taken care of every single immediate physical need the fire victims had. From food and water to diapers and baby formula, we had it covered. The Red Cross actually had to turn people away because they didn't know what to do with all the donations they were receiving from our church members.

A couple of days later, our local Fox affiliate did an update on the fire and its victims. The reporter, who had no connection with our church, told the audience that if they wanted to help the victims of the fire, they should call The Stone. Not the Red Cross or FEMA, but our church. The eyes of Austin were watching, and we seized the opportunity to serve those in need by letting the light of the gospel shine before them.

How Long, O Lord?

Aaron and Jamie Ivey are longtime partners at The Stone. Aaron is one of our worship pastors and a good friend of mine. In 2007, Aaron and Jamie adopted Amos, a one-year-old born in Haiti. Because of broken governmental agencies and poorly designed and executed administrative systems, the Iveys' efforts to bring their son home was an excruciatingly long process. The Iveys suffered setback after setback for more than two years, and when 2010 rolled around there was still no end to the process in sight.

Then, on Tuesday, January 12, at around 5:00 p.m. local time, a catastrophic 7.0 magnitude earthquake struck just sixteen miles outside Haiti's capital, Port-au-Prince. The Haitian government reported that more than 200,000 people had been killed and more than 1,000,000 were homeless. The Iveys didn't know what had happened to Amos, and they prayed mightily that he was still alive.

Word finally arrived from Haitian officials that Amos was safe. Not long after this good news arrived, the Iveys got the call that Amos was finally coming home. After several heartbreaking false alarms over the years, the Iveys knew this was *the* call they'd been waiting for; and for the first time in years, they allowed themselves to experience the emotions of joyful expectancy. Separated for more than two years from the son they longed to see and hold, they were now seemingly moments away.

The Iveys left Austin headed for Orlando, Florida, where they were told they could pick up Amos. When their plane landed in Orlando, they met up with about forty other parents who were in the same situation as they were, eagerly awaiting the arrival of their children. But none of them expected that the process was far from over. They would have to bear another long and unexpected round of suffering as flight schedules and U.S. Customs processes and background checks delayed the moment these parents longed for—being united with their adopted children.

"At one point," says Aaron, "I looked at my phone and saw it was three in the morning. The crazy thing is that for so long it had been this giant ocean that was separating us from our son, and then we're in the airport and it was this wall, a physical wall that was separating us from Amos. We were literally feet away from him, with nothing but a door between us. It was one of the most painful and frustrating parts of our journey."

Exhausted and in need of physical and emotional relief, Aaron finally went to sleep on the airport floor. "I think the sleep was for me an outward expression of trusting God with everything in my heart. I was saying, 'God, I trust you with this whole thing. I trust you with my son.' I had to, because there was absolutely nothing I could do about any of it."

Aaron awoke to the sounds of stirring and activity. "Finally, a U.S. Customs agent came out and called us back to see Amos." The years of waiting, the years of agonizing delays and unrealized expectations had finally come to an end.

> When I saw him, I ran to him and picked him up and held him so tightly. It was an emotional moment, not just because I was holding and kissing my son, because I'd done that before in our visits to Haiti. It was an amazing emotional experience because at that moment I literally held in my hands the ful-

fillment of God's promise when he told us all that time ago, "Amos is your son; pursue him."

Finally, there was no one telling us to wait, telling us we couldn't have him yet. Our suffering was finally over, and his suffering was too. He had come from such a hard place. He's only four years old, but he has had four incredibly hard years. His suffering was over. He's no longer an orphan; he has a family. He's finally home with Mama and Papa. Forever.

The Iveys' story is a story that teaches us much about the gospel. Like Amos, we too were orphans, separated from our Father, with no end to the separation in sight. Like Amos, we needed a family. And like Amos we were adopted and brought home.

When Jesus came and suffered, it was for our benefit. As Isaiah prophesied, "With his stripes we are healed" (Isa. 53:5). The separation that kept us from relating to God as our Father came to an end with Jesus' life. Though the Iveys suffered in the process of bringing Amos home, it was not without purpose. God had called them to pursue the son they loved, and their suffering paled in comparison to the joy that was set before them, the joy of holding their son and bringing him into their family.

God has pursued and adopted us through the suffering of Jesus Christ. And now we belong to him. The church, his family of adopted sons and daughters, belongs to the Father. And in his family our suffering is never in vain. It is for our good. It can even be for the good of others as they watch our faith and see it tested and refined to better reflect the glory of God. Suffering well may be the most important way the church can speak into a hurting world. We have a chance to suffer *with* people and respond with compassion. And we have the chance to suffer *for* people, to bear the burdens of others so that they may receive a taste of the gospel.

Aaron sums it up so well: "I know that I've been adopted into God's family. I was once an orphan with no purpose, no aim; but God in his kindness saw me, changed my past, gave me a future, and changed everything about me. I've been adopted, and I want to reciprocate that in the way I live my life."

Conclusion

What's next for The Austin Stone? Well, since I've shared with you a bit about our heart for adoption in this chapter, I want to say that I'm sick of Hollywood having a greater voice for adoption than the church. It's ridiculous. There are several hundred orphans in the city of Austin, and there are several *thousand* people coming to our church every weekend. Do the math. Why are there children in our city who don't have families? Three years from now, we want *zero* orphans in Austin. How will we do that? I don't know. But we're going to raise awareness, we're going to keep the vision in front of people, we're going to get involved in the lives of hurting children, and we'll suffer *with* and *for* them and show the world the gospel at every turn.

The church should have the same vocation as our King. Our adoption into the family of God brings with it the benefits of salvation, including the faith to endure suffering and find joy and purpose in God's mysterious work. Because of the gospel and the example of Jesus' suffering and our faith in God's sovereign purposes, we do not have to resist our suffering with resentment and bitterness. We believe that God will have the final word. Have you suffered unjustly? God will settle that account. You can look for God's purpose in it, and even when it seems hidden, enjoy his presence with you in the midst of it as you trust him to provide for all of your needs through Christ.

If we want to love our cities well, we must learn to suffer well, believing the good news that because of Jesus' suffering, we now have purpose in this life as well as the assurance of a life far removed from the suffering of this world. We can enter into suffering—both our own and the suffering of others—armed with the power of eternal forgiveness and the hope that Christ's return will make all things new. We can suffer with and for our cities because Jesus suffered with and for us, giving us hope beyond our suffering. Let us point others to that same hope by suffering well.

CHAPTER 9

Confessions
(Darrin & Matt)

Darrin's Confessions

We at The Journey are not a perfect church. Not long ago I (Darrin) delivered what proved to be a very difficult sermon. It was *difficult* because it was far too *easy* for me to give.

I know that doesn't make sense. So let me explain what I mean.

I titled the sermon "Confessions," and that's exactly what it was. It was a chance for me to provide our people with a peek under the hood of this church we call The Journey. And it was a difficult sermon because the time had come for me to publicly own up to and repent of the many flaws of our church.

The sermon was hard to give because I was not just confessing on behalf of an organization; I was confessing my personal failures as a leader and a pastor. As anyone who has ever led a ministry or a team of any kind knows, leading others means that you, as the leader, reproduce yourself. In some way, every part of the organization bears your resemblance, sometimes in ways that are more obvious than others, but your stamp inevitably and undeniably becomes part of the organization's DNA.

In my "Confessions" sermon, I stood before our congregation and asked for forgiveness for the ways I had led our church into various dysfunctions, problems that we could no longer avoid addressing or avoiding with typical excuses: "We're a young church," or "We're growing too fast to keep up with all the change." And as difficult as it was to admit it, it was all too easy to recognize how my personal flaws, and in some cases overt sins in my life and leadership, led to similar dysfunctions in our leaders and the culture of our church.

Savior Complex

From the earliest days of The Journey I felt compelled by a desire to help people not only understand the power of the gospel, but actually to live a life of holiness, a life rooted in that power. There is nothing wrong with this motive; in fact, I believe this should be a primary motive for *every* pastor and church planter. My problem was not the desire to live out the gospel message; rather, it was that in my attempts to do this, I allowed several other impure motives to arise in my life.

For example, many of our interns, staff, and most of the leaders of our church began the work of ministry without being adequately prepared, theologically and personally, for the weight and the burdens they were being asked to carry. I assumed that if I just kept the guys close to me, they would somehow learn the ropes as we went along. So I kept people in positions of authority who should not have been in those positions. This, in turn, led to frustration for those who were being inadequately cared for by underprepared leaders, and it led to painful disappointments for the leaders — men who had the right motives for ministry and even some natural gifts and skills, but who were continually failing because they lacked experience and training.

Self-Protection

Another sin I recognized in my ministry was the sin of self-protection. Self-protection is a sin rooted in pride. "Self" sins are always somehow associated with our pride. Consider the following "self" sins:

- Self-righteousness is trying to attain right standing with God by what you do instead of relying on what Christ has done on your behalf.
- Self-sufficiency is trying to live in your own strength instead of God's strength.

- Self-pity is believing that God owes you a better life instead of acknowledging that you owe God everything.

Self-protection, just like these other "self" sins, is rooted in our pride because it involves holding back part of who you are from other people because you fear rejection. This is a pride-rooted sin because it is really about choosing to get your security, your sense of self—your identity—from someone or something other than God.

I remember a key moment when I first realized that this sin was at work in my own heart. I was with our campus pastors in Louisville, Kentucky, visiting one of our sister churches in the Acts 29 Network.[1] During my visit I began to notice that the pastors and other staff and leaders at this church didn't just have professional relationships; they were also close personally—pursuing hobbies together and regularly gathering their families together to have dinner and hang out.

As I was having dinner with our campus pastors, I commented on what I'd seen earlier that day. "Did you guys notice how they are all friends? They all hang out together and do stuff with each other." They all had noticed it too. Then I asked a question that was intended to challenge and convict the campus pastors about their failure to not pursue more intentional relationships with each other.

I looked each man in the eye and asked them, "Guys, why don't you live like that?"

There was a brief silence as the importance of my question sank in. Finally, one of them responded.

"It's because of you, Darrin. *You* are the problem here. *We* do live like that, or at least we try to. Why don't you?"

I don't know if you've ever had one of those times where God reveals *both* your sin *and* its root in one flash of a moment, but that's what happened right then. And I was immediately convicted. Suddenly, it all started to make sense.

I was the problem.

---

1. Learn more about Sojourn Community Church by visiting www.sojourn church.com.

Right there in the restaurant, I started to cry, which isn't necessarily foreign to me, but it's not my country of origin either, if you know what I mean. I cried for about an hour, as God confronted me through these men about my sin of self-protection. God showed me that there was a thread that ran all the way through my life, beginning with my dad, who I had expected would be there to protect and provide for me and ended up leaving us instead. I thought about the coaches I'd had and how they should have seen a troubled young man without a dad, but instead saw just a talented athlete whom they could use for their purposes, not really investing into my life. I thought of how after I had become a Christian, pastor after pastor, mentor after mentor promised to be there for me, to help and guide me; yet they were never there when the rubber hit the road.

I remember sitting around that table with these fellow leaders and friends and confessing that I had shut them and others out of my life because I was afraid that they would leave me too, just as I had experienced time after time in my life. Over the years I had learned to become less open about my life and more protective.

And there were reasons for this as well. To be honest, I was absolutely unprepared for the sin and the problems I encountered when I first planted The Journey. Early on, it seemed as if every other woman I talked to had been sexually abused. I met with couples whose marriages were in terrible shape, couples who had been married five years and had yet to consummate their marriage. I had never experienced this level of brokenness before. I had never experienced the pain of shepherding and loving and leading someone, only to have them leave, lie, and gossip about me. I had come into the church plant theologically and spiritually prepared, but I was completely unprepared emotionally to deal with people at this level of brokenness.

And so I protected myself by withdrawing into some safe boundaries, and my sin of self-protection was now hurting the church. I wasn't fully giving myself to others, and I had chosen, over time, to compartmentalize my life and establish some unnecessary distinctions between my family life and professional life. To be clear, we all need to draw boundaries and protect our personal and family time and not become workaholics. I get all that.

But the truth is that we must also avoid an even more dangerous error—compartmentalizing our lives. The gospel destroys compartmentalization in our lives because the gospel demands all of us—not parts of us at different times. Because Jesus is indeed Lord of all, there is no room to hide parts of yourself from him, and the importance of this type of wholeness and integrity is even more of a necessity in vocational ministry. As I pulled away from those I was leading, I was removing myself from relationships with people, leaving them leaderless and reinforcing the lie that leading at The Journey was "every man for himself." I also saw how I had missed countless opportunities to receive blessing and encouragement from others—a value I had preached about and championed nearly every week.

Overpromise, Underdeliver

Another leadership failure I recognized was that I had set up an overpromise, underdeliver culture. Since I tend to be highly visionary, I like to talk about the future as if it has already happened. Now, the gift of vision can be a good thing. I can often see possibilities that few others see and effectively discern good opportunities from bad ones. But when you consistently tell people you are going to do something and then consistently fail to deliver it, you can no longer excuse it by telling people you're a "visionary." You are breaking the ninth commandment and lying to them. I hate to admit it, but I frequently lied to our congregation by making promise after promise, telling them how we were going to fix this problem or offer that class or provide this resource ... and then failing to deliver the goods.

You can probably begin to guess how this hurt our church. People felt as if they had gotten burned, time and time again. They began to lose trust in me and in our leaders, a huge problem at a large, elder-led church. In an elder-led church trust is vital because people don't involve themselves in all the details; rather, they trust their pastors with key decisions regarding the direction and execution of ministry.

The same is often true as a church becomes larger, regardless of its leadership structure.[2] As a church grows, the one-to-one accessibility that people have with key leaders decreases. This is not necessarily a bad thing; it is simply a reality for large churches. And in this environment trust is absolutely necessary if you want to mobilize people and keep them on mission. If they don't trust you, they won't follow you. If you consistently promise things that don't come true, you undermine your authority and weaken their commitment to the mission of God.

Antimeeting Culture

Before planting The Journey, I served with a pastor at another church who had a software engineering background. Not surprisingly, the meetings at his church were chock full of charts and graphs. Now, the only things I like less than charts and graphs are meetings *about* charts and graphs! In response to my previous experience, I was determined to make The Journey a "meet-only-if-absolutely-necessary" culture.

In the early days after our launch, our worship leader, Josh Dix,[3] and I would plan the service on a napkin at the South City Diner. The diner was not only my restaurant of choice, but it housed a booth that doubled as my office for the church for our first year. Other meetings typically consisted of my casting vision for fifteen minutes about my latest great idea and then telling people to go and make it happen. Not surprisingly, most of these visions failed because we didn't do the hard work of collaboration. I learned the hard way that when details are unclear, results are invisible.

This lack of meetings, fueled by my personal disdain for them, was hurting the church by creating chaos. It wasn't helping anyone. While I was trying to spare people from boring, corporate feeling meetings, I was actually deterring our leaders from valuing

---

2. Dr. Tim Keller provides excellent insights about the significance of a church's size contributing to ministry strengths and weaknesses in his article "Leadership and Church Size Dynamics." You can access the article free online at www.redeemer2.com/themovement/issues/2006/fall/church_size_dynamics.html.

3. Follow Josh's thoughts on ministry at joshdixonline.com

collaboration and contributing to clear communication among them. There was no sense of team. Our leadership "team" was actually a group of individuals doing ministry in isolation.

Discerning Good Opportunities from God Opportunities

I also failed to discern and distinguish *good* opportunities from *God* opportunities. Notice I didn't say good opportunities from bad opportunities. That is relatively easy. Distinguishing a good opportunity from a God opportunity is much more difficult. Usually, the difference is a matter of timing.

For example, when The Journey purchased property in the city of St. Louis, we were faced with the challenge of keeping the folks who were coming in from the suburbs on mission in their geographical area. The Sunday we opened our city campus I cast vision for a campus in the suburban West County area of the St. Louis metro area. We wanted to make sure people were going to a church near where they lived, not so much for their sake, but for the sake of their non-Christian friends who lived near them but would never consider going to a church in the city. The vision was right on, and the opportunity was there. The problem was not with the vision or the opportunity. I had simply ignored the issue of God's timing and when he might want this to happen.

I only recognize this now because hindsight is 20/20. When we started the West County campus, I thought it would be really simple. Re-create a worship service. How hard can it be? We'll stick a lay guy in charge, we won't devote any staffing resources, and I'll go pop in there on Sundays to yell at people and tell them what horrible consumers they are. They'll believe the gospel, the thing will grow, and everything will be fine.

Guess what? It was not fine at all. That campus struggled in a big way. And it is still struggling because we discerned the right opportunity, but we did not discern the right timing for the launch. I still believe that starting a campus in West County was the right thing to do. But the timing was wrong because we did not yet have a leadership structure that could sustain that kind of expansion. We should have waited. And though I believe our elders and campus leaders in West County will solve the problems and eventually make that campus an effective ministry center, by not discerning between a good opportunity and a God opportunity we've run into several problems and experienced ineffective ministry at that campus.

Focused on Ministry outside of The Journey

As the vice-president of the Acts 29 church planting network, I have had the great privilege of traveling the country assessing, training, and coaching hundreds of church planters. It has been a joy to watch God work through these men and their families to establish gospel-centered, missional ministry hubs in cities and small towns on both coasts and all in between. I am honored that God would use me and my experiences and insights to help churches be gospel lights in this dark world.

But there is a dark side to all of this. Yes, I traveled in order to help churches succeed. Yes, I traveled to connect pastors and church planters with other pastors and church planters so that no one had to go through the struggles of ministry alone. But if I am honest, there was always another motive behind much of my travel. Some of it was a chance for me to escape the leadership nightmares that were happening at The Journey.

Maybe a better way to say it is that I was abandoning the church one trip at a time so that I could "visit" another, less problematic world for just a little while. When I traveled, people valued me, they welcomed me, they saw me as wise and helpful. But at home, at The Journey, my flaws were exposed in every ministry we had started but not finished, every person falling through the cracks of our paths to service and community, every sermon that didn't "land" the way I wanted it to. So I filled my schedule with chances to escape. And the church suffered because I was not present to offer my best gifts in solving the problems, repairing the cracks, and honing my craft in preaching.[4]

---

4. I now submit all travel requests to the Executive Elder team at The Journey for their approval.

Consistently Violated the Sabbath

Along with this, I wasn't taking time away for rest and family. An interesting thing about the Sabbath is that we treat the command to honor it differently than we do the other commands. We don't say, "I may or may not commit adultery this week," or "I probably won't commit murder this week—but I might!" None of us would say that. And yet most of us have no problem making the command to honor the Sabbath optional. I was guilty of regularly disregarding this command for most of my time at The Journey. And it had negative effects on and in my body. I didn't get enough sleep. I had a string of stress-related illnesses that I will likely have to deal with the rest of my life. Worse than that, my wife and children suffered because of my lack of discipline in carving out quality time with my family.

Others suffered as well. I remember all too well the moment when God really convicted me of violating the Sabbath. I was in an elder meeting and Pastor Steve Miller was giving us a personal update as we prepared to pray for one another. His update turned into an emotional unraveling on full display for all the elders as he talked about his inability to get more than a few hours sleep a night, about the increasing frequency and intensity of migraine headaches, and about his lack of discipline regarding family time. As he shared this through tears, God spoke to me: "You did this to him. You did this with your crazy, nut job, workaholic, Sabbath-violating lifestyle. You call it persistence and perseverance, but it is sin, and this man who has been loyal to the gospel and this church is falling apart because he is imitating you."

I was ignoring the Sabbath, and the people connected to me were being hurt by it. I had consistently believed the lie that I was the one responsible to build the church, not Jesus. I regularly forgot that I was the creature, not the Creator. I ignored the reality that I did not have an infinite supply of energy, that I *must* rely on God as my source of strength because I am mortal and ravaged by the physical effects of living in a fallen world.

These were my "confessions." And even as I share them with you, I must confess that my struggles are not over. But those who seek to plant churches for the city, those who are passionate to proclaim the gospel and serve people, must start by looking within, at their own hearts, at their own failures and sins, and confess them, acknowledge them, and bring them out into the light.

Then, returning to the gospel, remember that in confession we find freedom and victory through what Jesus has done for us.

Matt's Confessions

While my [Matt's] sins and failings are many, there are two particular ways that I have failed as a planter and as a pastor. Both of these failures have created painful and, at times, devastating consequences for my wife, my children, and the many wonderful staff and laypeople at The Stone.

Unless you're walking with the Lord, genuinely being open to the Spirit's conviction, and welcoming of trusted family and friends confronting you, you are not likely to hear what I'm saying to you in the pages that follow. If you are like many planters/pastors, you have likely constructed your life in such a way that you cannot hear criticism or tolerate a touching of the brakes in your drive to success.

If this is you, then I'll say it plainly: you are a fool. I know this because I am the fool who committed my own mistakes. A wise person learns from the mistakes of others as well as his own. A fool cannot learn from others' mistakes, and so he condemns himself to make the same mistakes over and over again.

So let me say it one more time: if you can't read about my failures and learn from them, *you are a fool.*

Two of the biggest mistakes I made were burning out (overwork) and poorly leading my people. I did a horrible job of modeling what a healthy rhythm of life looks like to my staff and to our church body. And as a leader, I forced us to move too quickly, putting people into leadership too quickly. We were quick to hire and slow to fire with our staff and lay volunteers. As I describe both of my failures, I also want to follow up with some practical considerations that can help other pastors learn from these mistakes.

Burnout

The idea of *burnout* first came to my consciousness in 2006 at a Leadership Network learning community. I was involved in a small group with fifteen other young pastors, all about the same age. Matt Chandler, who had been the pastor of The Village Church north of Dallas for several years, also participated in a sister Leadership Network learning community of young pastors at the same time.

And when the two learning communities would meet in Dallas, we would gather at the same time, but in different rooms. At this time, Matt Chandler and I were just acquaintances, and we would talk in the lobby as the two groups were passing each other during breaks. For two years in a row we walked through the hotel lobby at the same time and almost every time we had a ten-minute conversation.

Chandler was preaching four services at the time, and I was preaching two. Matt told me a story about how he had preached for several weeks in a row, four times a Sunday, and how he eventually just came to the end of himself. He was just *done.* Empty. And he knew it had gotten really bad when, after finishing his fourth sermon that day, he went out to his car and started crying.

Now, I've got a sense of humor and I love to laugh and playfully haze friends in my life, and they dish it right back. So when this tall, lanky guy told me that after the fourth sermon he had slunk out to his car to have a cry, it was all I, the Aggie Corps guy, could do to keep from laughing and saying, "Wimp!"

Then, two years later, in 2008, I found myself also preaching four services a week. At the time, I was preaching through a vision series called "For the City." This sermon series was the result of the vision the Lord had given me to lead our people to serve our city. It was more than a sermon series or the kickoff for a new program or a fund-raising effort for a building. This was the vision the Lord had given me for our future — the vision of who we were to *become.* The For the City series transformed my life and the life of our staff, eventually changing who we were as we lived and worked and played Sunday through Saturday.

Every Sunday I would preach my heart out and then three to four nights a week I would spend time in the homes of different Austin Stone families and young adults personally casting the For the City vision. After about thirteen weeks (a little over three months) of preaching four services a Sunday, I left the facility one morning, walked out to my car, put the key in the ignition ... and started bawling like a baby. I couldn't stop crying. I didn't know *why* I was crying. I had seen my wife do something like this before, but it had never happened to me. I had no idea what was going on.

That Tuesday I went to my senior level staff meeting and stood up to tell them that I couldn't preach that Sunday because I had hit a wall. I got about a sentence into it and started crying. I don't remember how I got there, but I found myself on the floor crying uncontrollably. I had experienced complete exhaustion. My senior staff guys prayed for me and told me to go home. It was during this time that I remember thinking, "I'm not exactly sure what a nervous breakdown is, but I think I might have just had one."

I learned that I was suffering from burnout and was now living with the consequences of my unhealthy lifestyle decisions.

First of all, I now realize that I was preaching out of my talent and not out of the overflow of my walk with Jesus or from the anointing of the Holy Spirit.

Second, I had become numb to sin. I remember during week ten of the vision campaign when I came home one Sunday night after worship and my wife was asleep. I was exhausted. So I plopped on the sofa, clicked on the TV, and started flipping channels. Eddie Murphy's famously over-the-line comedy special from the '80s, *Raw*, came on. This was one of the first warning signs of my numbness to sin. Murphy's subject matter was *vile* and his language was obscene. A voice in my head recognized this reality, but I didn't care. I just didn't care. I remember thinking, "This is not healthy. Leave this. Get free," but I plowed through. I was so tired that I couldn't really hear the voice of the Spirit. And that's the principle I learned: when you're so tired that you can't hear or heed the Spirit anymore, you need to back off your work.

Both of these consequences also were affecting the church. When I was preaching out of my talent instead of the overflow of my walk and the Spirit's anointing, I was *robbing* the church of something precious. In addition, the model of Christianity I was presenting through my life, that I was something of a super-Christian who could handle anything, was unrealistic and unsustainable. Sabbath was an afterthought for me. My marriage was suffering. My fathering was suffering. And since I was pushing myself to the limits, I was also expecting my staff to push themselves to their limits. In various ways, some not so subtle, I had sent a message to my staff and to the church that I didn't need God. I had signaled, instead, that God needed *me*, that the church depended on *me*.

These mistakes have been some of the biggest—and most difficult—lessons for my life and in my ministry. I thank God for these lessons, but as you know, while the Lord is gracious to forgive sins, he doesn't always remove the consequences of our sinful choices.

What have been the consequences of my sins? For one, I burned out some wonderful, talented, gifted people who absolutely loved Jesus. I wish they were still with us, but sadly they aren't any longer. Back then I just saw them as weak. But as I think about it now, they weren't weak at all. They had families and jobs and struggles, and I was not leading them; I was driving them, like a herd of cattle.

At different times, I had communicated through nonverbal means and sometimes in my words, often behind their backs, "You're a loser. You're not tough enough." While I may have been gracious and understanding to their faces, privately I thought they were weak. I didn't realize the depth of my own arrogance and pride. And I didn't yet fully grasp my own weaknesses. I didn't fully recognize my need to stand on Jesus' blood and righteousness, and not rely on my own abilities, physical stamina, or good efforts to carry the day.

I wish I could say that there was an easy solution to this failure in my life, but to this day there is an ongoing tension for me and our staff: How can we lead our people—particularly our lay-people and volunteers—and not burn them out? We don't want to drive our volunteers too hard. We want to lead our people to unleash their gifts for God's glory. On the one hand, if we don't pull and encourage and nudge, many people will let the demands of their day job consume their time and gifts, leaving little time and energy available for other areas of service. On the other hand, however, if we push and cajole, we can drive too hard and hurt people. This is a tension that we continue to live with.

Leadership

When you plant a church and you've got twenty-five people or so coming, especially if your core team is 90 percent made up of college kids, you end up putting people into leadership who are not ready for leadership. In those early days, if you loved Jesus and were over age twenty-five and had a pulse, you were a leader at our church! To some degree, this was necessary, and it often worked great. In some sense, all of us were thrust into positions of leadership we weren't ready for.

That said, if I had to do it all over again, I would have significantly slowed down the initial planting process. It would have been better to let it grow more organically, and I would have been more cautious about putting people into positions of leadership, even if that meant letting the church grow at a slower rate. I now realize that the lack of time to allow people the opportunity to develop and mature kept us from having the right people in the right positions at the right stage of their life. Our needs were dictated by our programs, and we had more programs and ministries than we needed for our size and vision.

Unfortunately, these were lessons I could have learned from a book. Most of us don't like to admit this, but most church planters believe, at some level, that numerical growth is the definition of their success. *But numerical growth is not the definition of success.* However, because deep in our hearts we believe that numerical growth indicates success, we sell our souls and the souls of our people to get it. If, as a church planter, you can avoid getting caught up in the numbers game, you might actually be able to do it right the first time!

Unfortunately, in my case there were no books, seminars, or talks that could have aligned my heart with the truth. God had to take me *through* the idolatry and *through* the consequences of my idolatry. I had to be broken and repentant in order to learn these lessons. Still, I write this to you — as a pastor, lay leader, or future leader in the church — to plead with you to avoid the idolatry and the mistakes I made.

But there is a good chance you won't.

The reason is simple: even as I write this, you don't believe me in your heart! You *should*. You *need* to let go of the idol of growth. But because you won't let it go, you will end up hurting some really good people in your life. There will be people whom you want to love well, but will hurt deeply as you sacrifice their lives on the altar of success, pursuing numerical growth for your church.

Could It Have Been Different?

Did people try to articulate a healthier way of living as we were making these mistakes? Did the elders try to lead us in a different direction at times? Yes. For example, one elder waved the banner of Sabbath, arguing that we had to take a long-term, thirty-to-forty-year view of the ministry. He encouraged us to see our ministry at The Stone as a marathon, not a sprint.

In this same vein, an elder from another church who was mentoring our leaders used a different metaphor. He said, "You need to see your church as an oak tree, not as a squash. A squash has one root, grows only to a shallow depth, bears one fruit, and dies. But an oak tree grows slowly, putting down many deep roots, and it bears fruit for generations."

I now see how true this is. That's why I want to say to you again, as a church planter: as tempting as it may be, don't lead your church the way I did! Be wiser. Learn from my mistakes. You have to ask yourself whether you have made an idol out of the approval of others. Does your sense of value come from the size of your church or the notoriety of your name, or are you actually getting your value from your inclusion in Jesus Christ?

Jeremiah labored for forty years and never saw any fruit from his work. He was a voice crying in the wilderness. No one heard him, no one believed him, and no one turned from their sin. But Jeremiah did what he did because the Lord called him to do it.

So here's the question we must all answer in our hearts and with our lives: If the Lord came to you and said, "You're going to preach for forty years, you're never going to see any fruit, you're never going to make any money for your family," would you do it? Would you still be faithful to the call of Jesus? Is Jesus enough for you? If you can't answer that with a "yes," you need to quit the ministry and go sell insurance.

One of the resistances leaders have to hearing the call to repent of the idols of approval and success is a deceptive lie—that they are supposedly "giving their lives for Jesus." The greatness of the cause—the advance of the kingdom and the lifting up of Jesus' name in all areas of life—can unintentionally incline our hearts to serve idols in the name of "the cause." The mission can unwittingly become nothing more than God-talk that justifies our slavish devotion to the idols of approval and success.

From the beginning, my prayer has been, "Lord, you do something so powerful, so big that we *have* to attribute the work to you." I want to believe on my deathbed that Christ did the work, not me. On my deathbed I want to know: Did I pastor in such a way that I lived trusting in the Lord? Did I trust in the Lord enough to rest? Did I trust the Lord enough to delegate, to encourage my people to use their gifts? Did I trust in the Lord enough to put my wife and children first? Did I trust in the Lord enough to be small and insignificant?

What keeps me up at night is John 6. In John 6, Jesus was at the height of his popularity. He had just fed 5,000 men (likely at least 10,000 people, including the women and children). When you can gather a crowd of 10,000 to 15,000, you're a rock star. Jesus was a rock star in the ancient world.

All of this took place around the Sea of Galilee. When Jesus went from one side of the Sea to another, the crowds followed. They loved him! That is, until he offended them with the truth. After days of being followed around by the crowds, Jesus said to them, "You're just here because you ate a loaf of bread and were filled. But unless you eat my flesh and drink of my blood you have no part with me."

After that, the crowd abandoned him. Jesus basically ran off everyone but his core followers — the twelve disciples.

In this passage, Jesus reminds us that we're not called to be rock stars. As leaders in the church, we've got to be willing to preach truth. And if you and I are living to pass the next growth barrier instead of living for Jesus, we're missing the heart of the gospel.

So preach the truth, proclaim the good news about Jesus, and let your identity be rooted in his love for you. May your ministry avoid the idol of approval and the craving for success. Instead, may all that you do flow out of a heart broken by God's mercy and filled with his love, overflowing with grace as you preach the truth to your people and reach your community with the gospel.

CHAPTER 10

Conclusion:
Live Like Jonah
(Darrin & Matt)

So, let's say you're a Christian. Maybe you even live in a city. You've just read this book and are wondering what comes next. What, if any, practical steps can you take to encourage yourself, your family, your friends, and your church to be a church *for* your city? First, let me assure you that it's not all up to you. God has to do some great things *in* you before he will do something great *through* you. Your sin must be revealed to you and God's grace must be relished.

If we could choose just one person from the Bible to help us understand what it means, practically, for followers of Christ to be *for* our cities, we would suggest that you need to look no further than Jonah.

If you want to be *for* your city, be like Jonah.

Do you think your calling is difficult and your city is a rough place? Imagine being called to pronounce judgment on the capital city of the most powerful and violent superpower of the day. Consider what it would be like to preach a message of repentance to a nation where conquering soldiers ripped babies out from the bodies of pregnant women from the nations they defeated. Imagine what it would feel like to preach forgiveness to a nation that encouraged tossing children against rocks, brutally killing them.[1]

Even from a nation founded by a guy named Nimrod, this is worse than what most of us can imagine. Welcome to Nineveh-Assyria, prophet Jonah.

---

1. Assyrian war tactics are noted in Hosea 13:16 and Nahum 3:10.

About eight hundred years before Christ, Jonah prophesied to Israel, calling them back to covenant faithfulness (cf. 2 Kings 14:25). Jonah (whose name means "dove") seems to be a pure-hearted and well-intentioned prophet. He was gentle-hearted, but he was also the son of truth.[2] Like Elijah, Elisha, Hosea, and Amos, Jonah focused on uniting a nation that was divided because of sin and living under God's judgment. As a prophet, his calling was to bring awareness to Israel, teaching them that straying from God would be their end, while reminding the people that God was faithful to restore relationship with those who turned back to him and repented from their sin. Jonah gave his life for the health of his people. He prayed fervently for purity for himself and his people. His greatest dream, the thing that kept him up at night and got him out of bed in the morning, was a vision of his nation coming back to God.

Jonah loved his people. He loved them too much.

Jonah the Rebel

"'Arise, and go to Nineveh.'... But Jonah rose to flee ... from the presence of the Lord" (Jonah 1:1–3).

There is no clearer example of outright rebellion in the whole Bible than this passage. God says to go east, so Jonah hops a ship going west to the farthest known place on the map, a city in what is now known as Spain. Granted, God's call to Jonah was a little unusual for a Hebrew prophet. God basically said to him, "Jonah, go preach grace to your enemy nation, a nation that has already attacked your beloved nation three times."

Upon receiving God's command, Jonah immediately refused to obey, likely because he felt it was illogical and unwarranted. Jonah is the only prophet in the Old Testament called to speak to a pagan nation *on said pagan nation's soil*—an overtly hostile nation at that. Jonah's call was a missionary calling to a pagan nation, an unprecedented command of God in the Old Testament.

---

2. In Jonah 1:1 we learn that Jonah is the son of Amittai, which means he was the son of truth or faithfulness.

Nevertheless, Jonah's response was undeniably rebellious. Yet God responded to Jonah's self-righteous, nation-of-Israel-worshiping, comfort-preferring rebellion by refining the prophet through his saving grace and then calling him to preach that grace to his enemies, teaching Jonah that he deserved God's mercy about as much as they did.

Throughout the book of Jonah, God peels back the layers of Jonah's heart like a chef peels an onion. As layer after layer is removed, God exposes more of the waste product in Jonah's heart, and we, the readers, are witnesses to all of it. Through Jonah, God speaks to the ugliness of our own rebellion while pointing us to the fruit that God can produce, even in a prideful person, one who is willing to listen to God and obey his Word. For Christians with a desire to love our cities with the gospel, Jonah provides an example of the things we should avoid and illustrates some of the principles we should embrace as we seek to become God's gospel heralds in our cities.

Jonah's Rebellion Exposed

When Jonah first rebels against God's call, he takes a ship to Tarshish—the last point on a journey to nowhere. Up until this point, it is likely that Jonah felt pretty good about his life, his calling, his obedience to God. He probably thought of himself as a fairly righteous, faithful, and moral person. After all, he wasn't just a God-acknowledger or a God-follower; he was a God-proclaimer! He was a prophet, God's spokesman, the embodiment of God's message and vision to the world. He had always done what God had asked him to do. Until now.

What does Jonah's rebellion teach us?

Jonah's rebellion teaches us that if we want to be effective missionaries in our cities, we must see and recognize our own rebellion, our unwillingness to obey God. In other words, we can't help people see and repent of their own rebellion if we are not willing to see and repent of our own.

But not only must we see our rebellion, we must own it and

turn from it. Better yet, we should be *owning* it and *turning* from it frequently. Instead of aiming to be a person who *has* repented, aim to be a person who repents and is repenting. The humility required to develop a platform for the gospel comes from actively owning and consistently repenting of sin. Likewise, the confidence required boldly to address the ugliest, most broken parts of our cities comes as we actively embrace our forgiveness and identity in Christ.

In order to reach our cities, we need a fresh revelation from God—a revelation of our own wicked rebellion against him and our own wondrous acceptance in Christ! Humility and confidence comes from embracing the gospel of Jesus Christ, and it is the first thing that is required if we are going to effectively impact our cities.

Jonah's Prejudice Exposed

Jonah was a good Israelite, just as many of us are good Americans. He attended corporate worship and fellowshiped with people who shared his ideals and possessed a common vision for how the world should be. It is likely that Jonah had never really spent much time with people who didn't act like him, believe like him, behave like him, or even look and smell like him.

Until now.

God called Jonah to preach to the Assyrians. First of all, and most significantly for a Jewish man, the Assyrians were a different race. They were not Jewish. So, not only were they sinners, they were sinners who were not Jewish—part of God's chosen people. Jonah hated them because they were different.

After Jonah's rebellious choice to hop a ship to Tarshish, he found himself in a boat brimming with the fine, fresh scent of fish guts and sailor BO. The stench from this potpourri of smells proved almost as nauseating to him as the sailor's pagan beliefs. But Jonah didn't go all monotheistic on these guys who had a god for everything in creation: sun, moon, stars, and sea. Instead the only sound coming from Jonah's prophetic mouth was loud snoring. Jonah was fast asleep in the bottom of the boat in the middle of a storm.

God put Jonah in the midst of a serious situation with seriously broken people, and he slept. He appeared totally content to disengage. In fact, only after he was awakened from his slumber and was asked a specific question did he say anything about who God was to them.

What does Jonah's prejudice teach us?

Lest we get too judgmental on Jonah, we should realize a couple of important things. First, racism is a problem in every city, and it is an impediment to the gospel. This is true in Austin and St. Louis, and it's true in your city as well. If you aren't bringing the gospel to bear on this reality in your church and ministry, you are sinfully ignoring the elephant in the room. The church of God is to be a place where diversity is on display. Why? So that people will visibly see that it is not ethnicity or income bracket that unifies the people in your church, but the Spirit of Christ.

You may say, "But my all-white church reflects my all-white neighborhood. Isn't that the goal? Isn't that contextualization?" It may sound like a good excuse, but it's likely that you are not asking the next important question: "Why is my neighborhood all-white? What besides the gospel is unifying people here, and how does the gospel address and tear down that idol?"

We've also found that most of us can become extremely content just living in the midst of broken people and broken cities without purposefully entering into the mess and brokenness. We might speak up for God, but only if we are asked to do so. The church in the West has drawn people *into* the church, but it has done a poor job of *sending* them back out into the messy world. The result of all this is that the average new Christian will have virtually no non-Christian friends a mere two years after conversion. This is appalling! Our prejudice against non-Christians has pulled missionaries out of the context in which they are likely to have the greatest influence.

What all of us need, especially those who are motivated to be missionaries in their cities, is a fresh infusion of courage that empowers us to speak for God. We need to be reminded of our true identity in Christ, which liberates us from our ethnocentric and economic preferences and makes us more like Christ, who was a "friend" of sinners (Matt. 11:19; Luke 7:34). If the church is to bring the gospel's influence into our cities, we can no longer settle for just living in our safe little cocoon—even if it's located in the middle of the city. As we (Darrin and Matt) have stated throughout this book, if Christians and our churches are going to reach our cities for Christ, we must be *for* our cities, seeking their benefit and making friends with the sinners in our cities.

Jonah's Self-Righteousness Exposed

Jonah's attitude toward Nineveh and the Assyrians was, shall we say, less than loving. He was, by textbook definition, *against* this city. He saw the Ninevites as dirty, rotten pagans undeserving of God's mercy and completely deserving of God's wrathful judgment. It is shocking to read of Jonah's rebellious contempt for Nineveh, especially considering the fact that God called Nineveh an important, strategic city (Jonah 1:2; 3:2–3).

Another surprise comes when Jonah made an outright confession in 4:2 that the sin underneath his rebellion, apathy, indifference, and conditional obedience was self-righteousness: "That is why I made haste to flee to Tarshish; for I knew that you are a gracious God and merciful, slow to anger and abounding in steadfast love, and relenting from disaster."

Wow! Jonah essentially says two things here. First, and most apparent, Jonah says, "I didn't want to go to that wicked city because I was afraid that you would forgive them." Then, a bit more indirectly, he says, "I don't think they deserve grace like we (Jonah and Israel) do."

As the narrative unfolds, it becomes clear that not only is Jonah more impressed with Israel's faithfulness to God than God's favor to Israel, Jonah is more impressed with his own commitment to God than God's commitment to him. Jonah's theology looks something like this: "I earned God's grace with my good life and

I'm content to let others do the same. If they don't have a good life, then they deserve God's judgment."[3]

What does Jonah's self-righteousness teach us?

Churches *for* their city will preach hard against self-righteousness. Self-righteousness cultivates a classic "Us vs. Them" mentality, an attitude that is all too prevalent in the Western church. As we see in Jonah's story, self-righteousness is dangerous because it keeps us from truly entering into the lives of people in the city because we think we are better than they are. Self-righteousness makes our message unattractive because it communicates to the people we are trying to reach with the gospel that they are inferior to us.

How do we preach against our self-righteousness? We simply preach the gospel. The gospel, rightly comprehended, puts every person on equal footing. None of us deserves God's favor; instead, we all deserve God's wrath. Preaching the gospel reminds Christians that they *have done* nothing to earn salvation and alerts non-Christians to the fact that they *can do* nothing to earn it.

If we are going to learn from Jonah and build an effective platform for the gospel in our cities, we need to preach continually the biblical perspective of salvation: that we are right with God because of Christ, not because of our "morally superior" lives.

Jonah's Comfort-Seeking Exposed

Jonah eventually obeyed God, though begrudgingly, and called Nineveh to repent. He then left the city, hoping that the Ninevites would not heed his message and that God would judge—that is, destroy—the city (Jonah 4:5).

Hypocritically, Jonah then committed the same sin that contributed to Nineveh's impending judgment. As it turns out, Jonah loved his own comfort more than God. He made a little shanty to shield himself from the heat of the sun. Then he enjoyed the shade

---

3. This may have been behind Jonah's willingness to be thrown out to sea in 1:12. Jonah believed that he deserved to die because of his lack of obedience.

of a plant that God provided for his protection.[4] When the plant was removed, Jonah wanted to die. In other words, Jonah reveals that he was not living for the fulfillment of God's purposes in Nineveh, but for his own personal comfort.

What does Jonah's comfort-seeking teach us?

Rather than finding security and comfort in God and in God's calling, Jonah has committed the fundamental sin of the human heart—worship of an idol. G. K. Beale says, "Whatever your heart clings to or relies on for ultimate security is your object of worship."[5] In this instance Jonah worships the idol of comfort. Ultimately, Jonah prefers to maintain his own comfort more than he longs for the salvation of a troubled (and troubling) city.

- Worshiping comfort, Jonah loved a plant while God loved the city.
- Worshiping comfort, Jonah sought personal pleasure while God sought the hearts of people.
- Worshiping comfort, Jonah desired Nineveh's judgment while God extended Nineveh grace.

Lest we be too hard on Jonah, possibly the biggest temptation many of us face is all too similar. We are content to simply be *with* our city rather than *for* our city. It is difficult to live in a city and remain uninfluenced by the idols of that city. Though every city manifests idolatry in unique ways, each of us is tempted to love comfort more than God. It is our fallen sinful nature to desire an unbothered, unchallenged, hassle-free, responsibility-free life. We all desire to put our life on cruise control and coast at a pace that suits our own personal agenda.

But if we want to be a church for our city, we must radically trust God to liberate our imaginations from the idol of comfort. We need to do more than just recognize God as our true source of comfort. Our entire lives must be seized by God's purposes in

---

4. This plant was probably a castor oil plant or a gourd plant, both of which have large leaves.

5. G. K. Beale, *We Become What We Worship: A Biblical Theology of Idolatry* (Downers Grove, IL: InterVarsity Press, 2008), 17.

us and in our churches. Until God replaces our desire for self-centered comfort with a desire for other-centered service, we will be slaves to the idol of comfort. And God will not change our hearts until we lay down our idol. When we, with God, seek the welfare of our cities, we will not be satisfied with the pleasures of our culture but will rest only in the treasure Christ himself.

Jonah *For* the City

The book of Jonah ends with a question. God asks, "Should not I pity Nineveh, that great city, in which there are more than 120,000 persons who do not know their right hand from their left, and also much cattle?" (Jonah 4:11). The question is left unanswered for Jonah to wrestle with it. And so should we. We must ask ourselves, "Should I not be moved and grieved for my city with so many spiritually lost and wandering people? Should I not be more concerned for the spiritual condition of people than the prizes of status and wealth in my culture?"

In a backward sort of way, we actually know that Jonah *did* answer the question God put to him, and that he got the answer right. We know Jonah got it right because he penned the words of the book. Though he blew it with Nineveh, Jonah was ready to be *for* the next city to which God called him. By ending the book with a question, Jonah shows us that for the rest of his life, he would preach grace to hurting people, no matter who they were, where they were, or what they were doing. I believe that five words found in his prayer from chapter 2, when Jonah was saved by God's grace, worked their way deep into his heart.

"Salvation belongs to the LORD," cried Jonah from the belly of a fish. Some have called Jonah 2:9 the central theme of the whole Bible. In a simple statement, these five words tell us everything we need to know about God and ourselves: Salvation belongs to the Lord.

Jonah came to understand that salvation did *not* come from his moral life, his ethnicity, or his calling as a prophet, but only from God. Jonah moved from thinking that grace was his right to seeing grace as an underserved gift from an unobligated giver. The text tells us that while he was trapped in the fish, Jonah was able to meditate on God's temple (Jonah 2:7). By meditating on the temple, Jonah was reminded that God's grace is both costly and free.

The temple represented both bad news and good news to the Israelites. The fact that the temple existed was a constant reminder of their sinful condition and their need for a sacrifice of atonement. The good news, however, was that the temple was visible proof that God dwelled among his people. The temple was a place of worship, a place where worship was acceptable through the sacrifices.

The physical layout of the temple teaches us a great deal about the spiritual implications of Jonah's meditation in the belly of the fish.

The temple contained altars of sacrifice. As noted in the illustration there was an altar of burnt offering and an altar of incense. These were altars on which the priests could offer sacrifices, which they regularly did as a customary part of Jewish worship.

Because of the people's sin, they were not allowed access to the most significant of the temple's altars. An inner chamber of the temple known as the Most Holy Place—the Holy of Holies—was where God's presence physically dwelled. Only the high priest could enter this chamber in the presence of God, and even he could enter but once a year on Yom Kippur.[6]

Within the Most Holy Place was the ark of the covenant, something of a treasure chest that likely contained Aaron's budded rod (a sign of the rebellion of God's people),[7] some manna (a sign of people's need to daily walk with and trust God),[8] and the

---

6. The holiest day of the Jewish calendar, Yom Kippur is known as the "Day of Atonement." On Yom Kippur, the high priest enters the inner sanctum of the temple and makes an animal sacrifice on behalf of himself and the Jewish people as a God-ordained way to atone for sin. See Leviticus 16 for Yom Kippur's origin and Hebrews 9 for a New Testament understanding of Christ's fulfillment of this Jewish holy day.

7. Numbers 17:8–11; Hebrews 9:4.

8. Exodus 16:32–34; Hebrews 9:4.

tablets of the Ten Commandments, the tangible display of God's moral law.[9]

Atop the ark was a golden slab upon which the high priest sprinkled the blood of the yearly animal sacrifice on Yom Kippur. The blood came from a "spotless" animal, slaughtered in order to atone for the sins of God's people. This is why the slab was called "the mercy seat"; it was the place where the blood of the innocent was exchanged for the mercy of God and the forgiveness of sin.

So keep in mind that beneath the mercy seat were the tangible signs of God's holiness (the tablets of the Ten Commandments) and the people's rebellion (the rod of Aaron). Side by side, God's holiness and the people's rebellion spelled doom for them, wrath and judgment.

Yet sitting above all of this was the seat of God's mercy. The same God who required perfect obedience to the law had also provided a substitute for their imperfect obedience. God's mercy would deliver God's people from God's righteous judgment.

God wants us, like Jonah, to live out our calling and our obedience based on the reality of his justice and mercy. Jonah had the temple. We have the cross.

At the cross we see where justice and holiness kiss and God's free but costly grace flows freely. Like Jonah we see God's demand for holiness: someone had to pay with his life for the sins of the people. Righteousness never comes without a cost. At the same time, on the same cross, we see God's mercy in that "while we were still sinners, Christ died for us" (Rom. 5:8).

As this good news shapes our thinking and our actions, it becomes the foundation for our identity as sons and daughters of this just and merciful God. With a new identity, rooted in what Christ has done, we can go into our cities with humility, laying down our self-righteousness because we know that we, like those we are called to serve, are sinners. But we will also take the gospel into our cities with confidence, without a shred of self-doubt, because we know that we are forgiven by God in Christ.

---

9. Exodus 20; 34:28; Deuteronomy 10:5; Hebrews 9:4.

Until we plumb the depths of our sin and embrace the full acceptance of God that is ours in Christ, we won't be for our cities.

Jesus didn't run from hard obedience, but ran to God in full obedience.

Jesus didn't run from his enemies, but ran to them.

Jesus wasn't just thrown into the depths for a few sailors, but for the whole world.

Jesus wasn't against the people, or simply with them or among them. He was *for* them, so much so that he gave his life *for* them.

If we are to be like Christ, we too must lay down our life for the sake of our cities.

We are Jonah.

We are Jonah because we are:

- a *rebellious* people
- a *self-righteous* people
- a *comfort-loving* people
- a *people-avoiding* people

But we are also Jonah because we are:

- a *redeemed* community experiencing the daily blessing of God's salvation
- a *strategically placed* community seeking God's purposes for our city
- a *countercultural* community with an unpopular but strangely attractive perspective on cultural idols like sex, power, and money
- a *called* community in possession of a dangerous message that God intends us to take beyond the walls of the church and into the lives of the lost

To understand grace is to know down deep that you have nothing to offer God but your uninspired, rebellious, disobedient life. The good news is that God delights in using broken people like us to reach broken cities like ours.

This calling to reach our cities is bigger than any of us. Contrary to popular belief, the notion that God will not put on us more than we can handle is unbiblical. God always calls us to do more than we can handle, and he does this in order to bring us back to him as the source of our strength and power. He lays supernatural tasks on us because he wants us to rely on him for supernatural strength.

Reaching our cities for Christ requires more courage, patience, strength, tenacity, and generosity than any church has. Our lack of resources and our limited capacity is why we desperately need God's Spirit.

So, as we close, consider this question: Are you living in a way that requires God's supernatural power for your calling to be lived out?

Are you taking the kinds of risks and dreaming the kinds of dreams that will never reach fruition unless God shows up and provides what is needed?

Your city needs to see radical, Jesus-inspired generosity. Are you radically trusting that God will provide when you are faithful to give? Is your church?

Your city needs relational evangelism and bold, clear proclamation of the gospel. Are you trusting God to show you when and what to speak and to whom? Is your church proclaiming the good news of Jesus' redemption in a way that actually redeems the best laid plans and misguided hopes of your culture?

Your city needs to experience Jesus-inspired compassion. Are you trusting God to reveal sin and selfishness in you and your church? Are you fully repenting of your sin by seeing it, owning it, and turning from it so that you can get your eyes off yourself and see the hurting and poor with Christlike compassion?

While much has changed since Bible times, at least one thing hasn't. Salvation belongs to the Lord. The gospel triumphs because Jesus is King. The gospel triumphs because Christ is the Victor. The gospel triumphs because Christ has died, Christ is risen, and Christ will come again. A church for its city is willing to dream big and take scary risks because the God who began a good work in and through the church is the God who will use the church to bless cities, nations, and the entire world.

Epilogue

Alan Hirsch

There is no doubt in my mind that if we have not already passed it, we are close to a system-wide tipping point in the evangelical church world today. This book itself is significant evidence that something elemental is happening in our day. Let me make my case...

In your hands is a book written by top-rate practitioners of what we know as the megachurch model. Matt and Darrin are passionate, intelligent, and deeply spiritual church planters who have amply demonstrated their leadership by starting churches from scratch and seeing them grow to where they have attendance of many thousands each weekend. In other words, if you were looking for textbook examples of how leadership and church planting should be done, at least according to the best thinking of the contemporary church approach, then you need not go much further than them. They embody success as most American evangelicals currently define it.

But they have not been content to rest on their supposed laurels. Fueled by a transformative vision of the world, they have begun to ask serious questions about impacting their neighborhoods and beyond that, whole cities, with the gospel. In order to do this they have had to fundamentally recalibrate their understanding of church based on both the ecclesiology and the incarnational approach to mission that is rooted in the New Testament itself. They are living into the New Testament understanding of missional church and they are beginning to experience some amazing fruits as a result.

I have a constant refrain now that goes something like this: that many of the problems that the church now faces can actually be resolved simply by thinking differently about the church and its God-designed mission in the world. In other words, by changing our metaphors and paradigms of church, we can change the game. The name I give to this different paradigm of church is "apostolic movement." The concept is not new; in fact, it's ancient, and it describes completely the fluidity and dynamism of the spiritual phenomenon we see evidenced in the pages of the New Testament itself. The Austin Stone and The Journey are now beginning to reframe themselves as movements, and they are unleashing the sheer power of New Testament ecclesiology as a result. This is the church as Jesus intended it to be ... a gospel-empowered, unfettered people movement, perfectly designed for nothing less than the transformation of the world and the destruction of the forces of evil (Matt. 16:18).

About the Authors

A longside worship leader Chris Tomlin, **Matt Carter** is the Senior Pastor of Austin Stone Community Church in Austin, Texas, one of the hundred fastest-growing churches in America with an average attendance of over five thousand people at their five services. Matt currently lives in Austin with his wife, Jennifer, and his three children, John Daniel, Annie, and Samuel.

Darrin Patrick is lead pastor of Journey Church in St. Louis, Missouri, which he planted in 2002 and currently has over three thousand people and five campuses. He is also the vice-president of Acts 29, a missional church-planting network. He has been married to his wife, Amie, since 1993; they have four children: Glory, Gracie, Drew, and Delainey. To stay connected with Darrin, visit *PastorDarrin.com*

Joel Lindsey is a writer and elder at The Journey in St. Louis, Missouri. He loves Jesus and enjoys bluegrass music. Joel and his wife, Melissa, have three sons. He blogs daily at *subvergent.com*.

Share Your Thoughts

With the Author: Your comments will be forwarded to the author when you send them to *zauthor@zondervan.com*.

With Zondervan: Submit your review of this book by writing to *zreview@zondervan.com*.

Free Online Resources at
www.zondervan.com

Zondervan AuthorTracker: Be notified whenever your favorite authors publish new books, go on tour, or post an update about what's happening in their lives at www.zondervan.com/authortracker.

Daily Bible Verses and Devotions: Enrich your life with daily Bible verses or devotions that help you start every morning focused on God. Visit www.zondervan.com/newsletters.

Free Email Publications: Sign up for newsletters on Christian living, academic resources, church ministry, fiction, children's resources, and more. Visit www.zondervan.com/newsletters.

Zondervan Bible Search: Find and compare Bible passages in a variety of translations at www.zondervanbiblesearch.com.

Other Benefits: Register yourself to receive online benefits like coupons and special offers, or to participate in research.

ZONDERVAN®

ZONDERVAN.com/
AUTHORTRACKER
follow your favorite authors